Homework H Science

Ages 8–9
Key Stage 2/Year 4

Andy Bailey, Jane Harris
& Michael Wilkinson

 *We're the Homework Helpers!*

 *We've thought up lots of fun activities for you!*

  *So grab your pens and pencils...*

 *...and let's get started!*

Longman

An imprint of **Pearson Education**

Harlow, England · London · New York · Reading, Massachusetts · San Francisco
Toronto · Don Mills, Ontario · Sydney · Tokyo · Singapore · Hong Kong · Seoul
Taipei · Cape Town · Madrid · Mexico City · Amsterdam · Munich · Paris · Milan

Series editors:
Stuart Wall & Geoff Black

With thanks to Jane Webster for additional material

These people helped us write the book!

A complete range of **Homework Helpers** is available.

		ENGLISH	MATHS	SCIENCE
Key Stage 1	Ages 5–6 Year 1	✓	✓	Science is not included in the National Tests at Key Stage 1
	Ages 6–7 Year 2	✓	✓	
Key Stage 2	Ages 7–8 Year 3	✓	✓	✓
	Ages 8–9 Year 4	✓	✓	✓
	Ages 9–10 Year 5	✓	✓	✓
	Ages 10–11 Year 6	✓	✓	✓

This tells you about all our other books.

Which ones have you got?

Pearson Education Limited
Edinburgh Gate, Harlow
Essex CM20 2JE, England
and Associated Companies throughout the world

© Pearson Education Limited 2000

The right of Andy Bailey, Jane Harris and Michael Wilkinson to be identified as authors of this work has been asserted in accordance with the Copyright, Designs and Patents Act 1988

All rights reserved; no part of this publication may be reproduced, stored in any retrieval system, or transmitted in any form or by any means, electronic, mechanical, photocopying, recording, or otherwise without either the prior written permission of the Publishers or a licence permitting restricted copying in the United Kingdom issued by the Copyright Licensing Agency Ltd, 90 Tottenham Court Road, London W1P 0LP.

First published 2000

British Library Cataloguing in Publication Data
A catalogue entry for this title is available from the British Library

ISBN 0-582-38153-3

Printed in Great Britain by Henry Ling Ltd, at the Dorset Press, Dorchester, Dorset

This is for grown-ups!

Guidance and advice

Schools are now asked to set regular homework, even for young children. Recent government guidelines for Year 4 (ages 8–9) suggest $1\frac{1}{2}$ hours of homework a week. Children are also encouraged to do at least 10–20 minutes of reading each day.

Experimental and investigative science

The aim of the National Curriculum for science is to develop children's knowledge of scientific ideas, processes and skills, and relate these to everyday experiences. Teachers provide opportunities for children to make predictions, plan experiments, learn how to make their test fair, record results, consider evidence, and then think about their results and the effectiveness of the experiment.

All the activities in this book are written to complement the National Curriculum. The emphasis is on short, enjoyable activities designed to stimulate a child's interest in science. Each activity will take 10–20 minutes, depending on the topic, and the amount of drawing and colouring.

Themes and topics

Throughout the book key words have been set in **bold** text – these highlight the themes and content of the activities, and provide a guide to the topics covered.

Encourage your child

Leave your child to do the activity on their own, but be available to answer any questions. Try using phrases like: That's a good idea! How do you think you could do it? What happens if you do it this way? These will encourage your child to think about how they could answer the question for themselves.

If your child is struggling …

Younger children might need help understanding the question before they try to work out an answer, and children who need help with reading or writing may need you to work with them. If your child is struggling with the writing, ask them to find the answer and then write it in for them. Remember, even if your child gets stuck, be sure to tell them they are doing well.

The activities start on the next page! Have you got your pens and pencils ready?

Check the answers together

When they have done all they can, sit down with them and go through the answers together. Check they have not misunderstood any important part of the activity. If they have, try to show them why they are going wrong. Ask them to explain what they have done, right or wrong, so that you can understand how they are thinking.

You will find answers to the activities at the back of this book. You can remove the last page if you think your child might look at the answers before trying an activity. Sometimes there is no set answer because your child has been asked for their own ideas. Check that your child's answer is appropriate and shows they have understood the question.

Be positive!

If you think your child needs more help with a particular topic try to think of some similar but easier examples. You don't have to stick to the questions in the book – ask your own: Did you like that? Can you think of any more examples? Have a conversation about the activity. Be positive, giving praise for making an effort and understanding the question, not just getting the right answers. Your child should enjoy doing the activities and at the same time discover that learning is fun.

More on Science

There are many activities you can do outside school that will help develop your child's familiarity with science and provide valuable practice. Make sure your child has plenty of experience of weighing, measuring, observing processes and making comparisons. Look for opportunities to help your child practise predicting what will happen, collecting evidence and recording results. The more practice your child gets the more comfortable with science they will become.

Where do they live?

A **habitat** is a place where animals and plants live.

1. Draw a line to match each living thing to its correct habitat.

A habitat is more than a home – it is a place that contains everything a plant or animal needs to live.

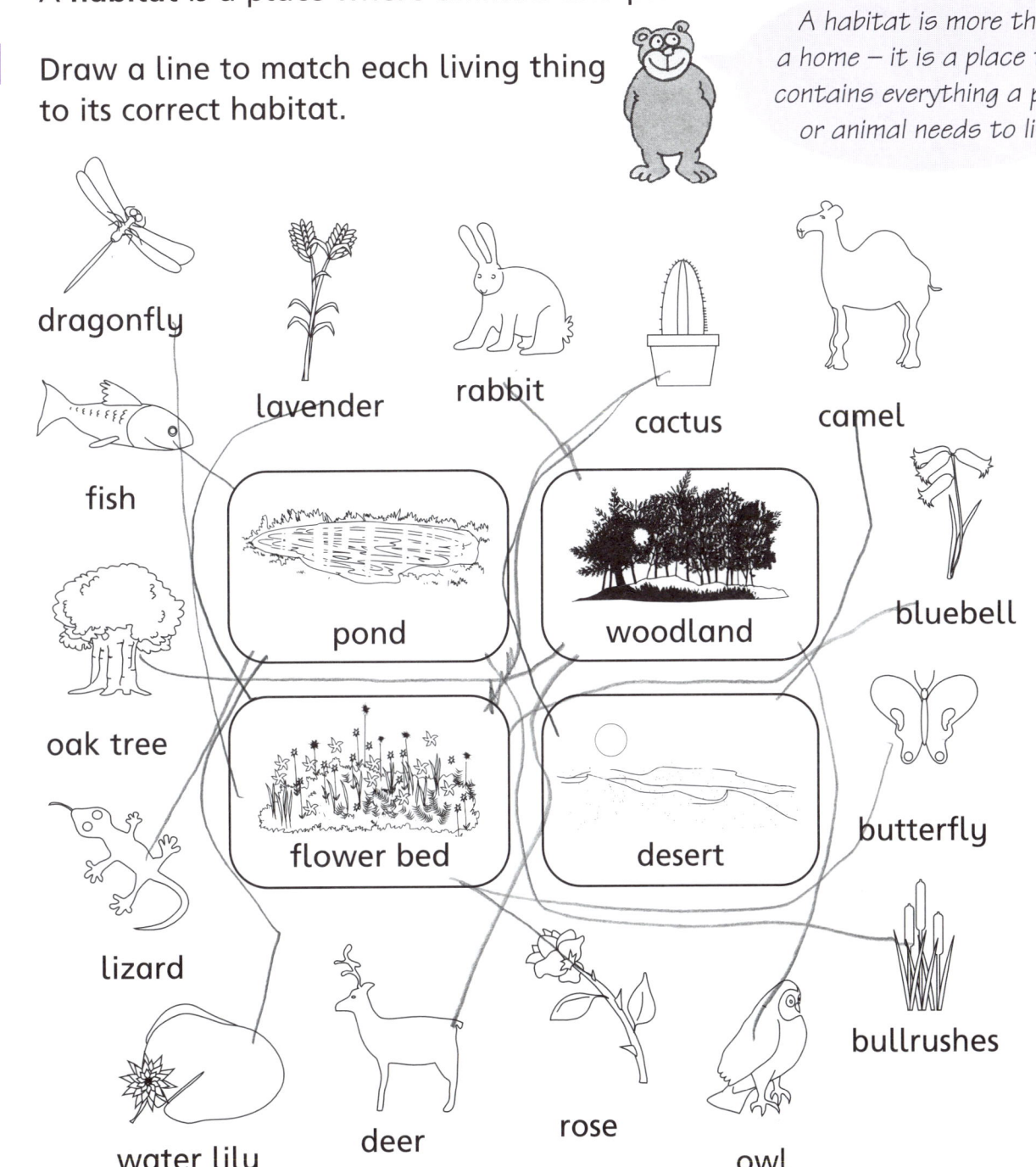

2. Write the names of other living things that live in these habitats.

_____

_____

Habitat conditions

Here are words which are linked with **habitats**.

shady, wet, shelter, food source, dry, damp, light, dark, protection

Words like dark, wet, shady, describe the conditions in the habitat.

Words like shelter and protection, are the benefits the habitat offers to living things.

1 Ring or colour the words.

s	f	o	o	d	s	o	u	r	c	e
p	h	x	l	i	g	h	t	r	z	z
r	t	e	d	k	w	y	l	e	s	y
o	k	d	l	y	b	b	u	f	w	c
t	m	a	r	t	g	s	e	e	w	a
e	q	r	w	x	e	h	w	s	j	c
c	h	k	t	p	e	r	a	h	q	r
t	w	e	t	m	i	p	i	a	w	b
i	h	a	k	p	n	e	m	d	h	f
o	r	o	d	r	y	e	z	y	x	f
n	l	j	d	f	m	n	d	a	m	p

Words can read across, down or diagonally.

2 Now use some of these words to describe the **conditions** of each of the habitats on the next page.

Some habitats have more than one condition, so use more than one word for these.

All living things find food, shelter and protection in their habitat.

under stones
dark
damp
~~soggy stuf~~

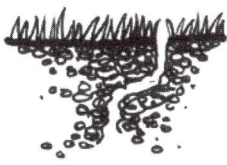
under the soil
wet ✗
dark ✓

on walls
dry ✓
light ✓

in long grass
wet
shelter

on leaves
good source
damp

in a pond
wet
protection

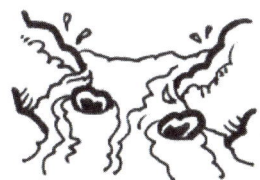
in a stream
light
wet

under logs
dark
shady
damp

on marshland
light
protection

Sorting animals

Vertebrates (animals with backbones) are sorted into five main groups.

The groups are: **fish**, **amphibians**, **reptiles**, **birds** and **mammals**.

1 These animals are all vertebrates. Which group does each animal belong to?

Write your answers in the boxes under the animals.

goldfish

sparrow

mouse

fish

bird

Mamal

frog

snake

The column for fish has been filled in for you.

ampibiants

reptile

2 Complete this table by ticking the correct boxes to describe each group.

	Fish	Amphibians	Reptiles	Birds	Mammals
Cold-blooded	✓	✓	✓		
Warm-blooded				✓	✓
Have moist skin		✓			
Have scales	✓		✓		
Have feathers				✓	
Have fur or hair					✓
Breathe through gills	✓	✓			
Breathe through lungs		✓	✓	✓	✓
Lay eggs	✓	✓	✓	✓	✓
Give birth to live young					✓

8

What am I?

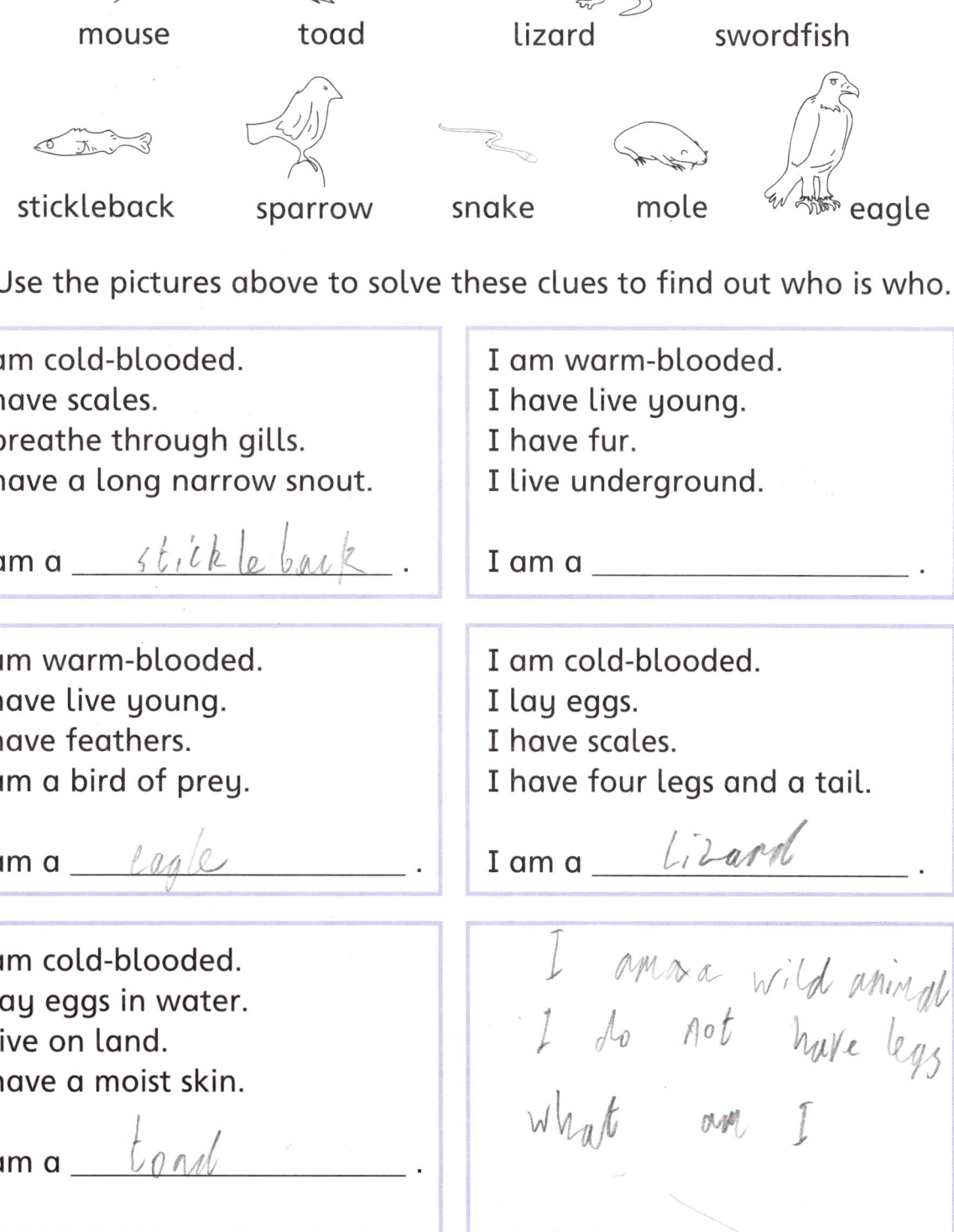

1. Use the pictures above to solve these clues to find out who is who.

I am cold-blooded.
I have scales.
I breathe through gills.
I have a long narrow snout.

I am a ___stickleback___.

I am warm-blooded.
I have live young.
I have fur.
I live underground.

I am a _____.

I am warm-blooded.
I have live young.
I have feathers.
I am a bird of prey.

I am a ___eagle___.

I am cold-blooded.
I lay eggs.
I have scales.
I have four legs and a tail.

I am a ___lizard___.

I am cold-blooded.
I lay eggs in water.
I live on land.
I have a moist skin.

I am a ___toad___.

I am a wild animal
I do not have legs
what am I

2. Now make up your own clues for one of the other animals, to test your friends or family. Write the clues in the empty box.

Sorting minibeasts

Minibeasts are **invertebrates** (animals with no backbone).

1. Write the names of these minibeasts in the correct place on the **Venn diagram**.

| minibeasts with legs | | minibeasts with wings |

This is a Venn diagram.

Does every place on the Venn diagram have names?

2. One minibeast will be outside the rings. Write its name in the box.

snail

3 Sort the same 12 minibeasts into the correct sections of this **Carroll diagram**.

	six legs	not six legs
wings	beetle ✓, moth ✓, bee ✓, wasp ✓, ~~spider~~, housefly ✓	~~spider spider~~, ~~bee~~ ladybird, dragonfly
no wings	woodlouse, millipede, earwig, ~~bee~~, ~~spider~~, ant, centipede	~~snail~~ snail, slug

4 Try to think of more minibeasts and write their names in the correct section of the Carroll diagram.

*Minibeasts which have six legs and three parts to their body are called **insects**.*

Minibeast sorting trees

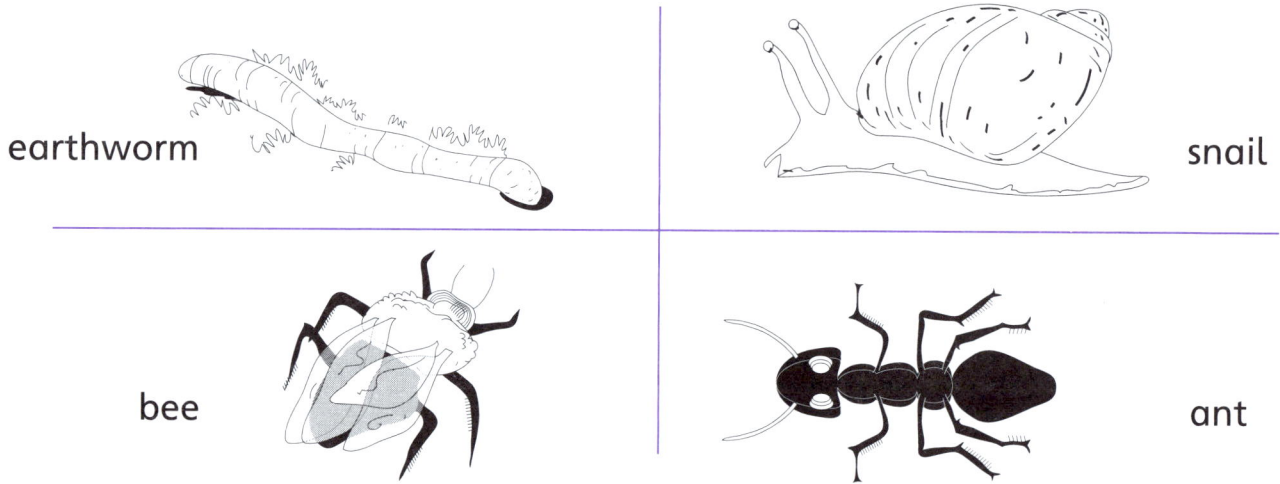

earthworm   snail
bee   ant

| Write the name of each of these minibeasts in the correct box at the bottom of the **sorting tree**.

Does it have legs?

This is a sorting tree. Answer the questions and follow the branches.

Yes — Does it have wings?
No — Does it have a shell?

Yes: bee
No: ant
Yes: snail
No: earthworm

2 Here are some more minibeasts. Complete the sorting tree by adding a question to each empty box.

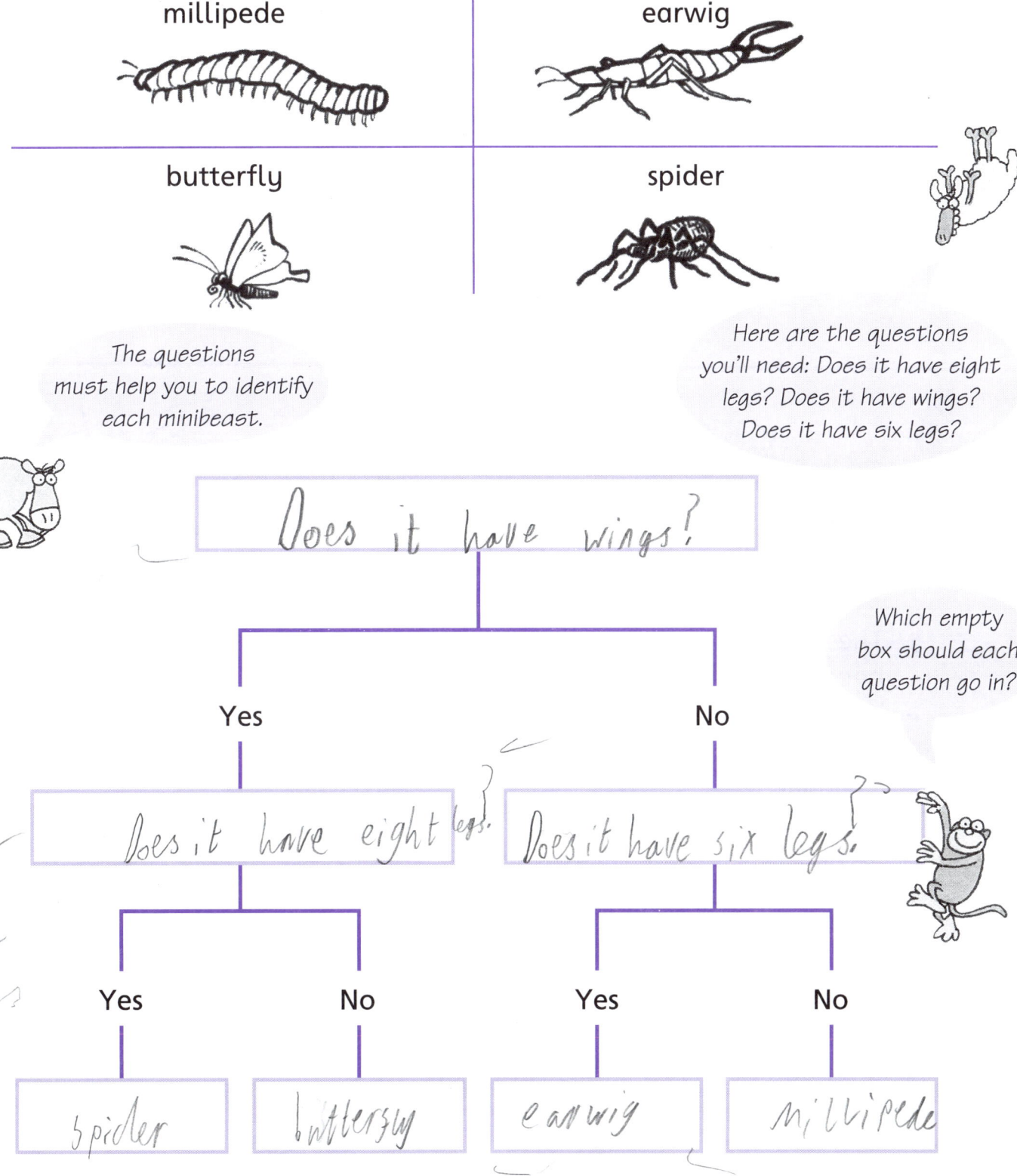

The questions must help you to identify each minibeast.

Here are the questions you'll need: Does it have eight legs? Does it have wings? Does it have six legs?

Which empty box should each question go in?

Top box: Does it have wings?

Yes → Does it have eight legs?
- Yes: spider
- No: butterfly

No → Does it have six legs?
- Yes: earwig
- No: millipede

3 Write the name of each minibeast in the correct box at the bottom of the sorting tree.

Food chains

All living things need energy. Plants get this from the Sun while animals get it from eating plants or other animals. A **food chain** shows how plants and animals get their energy and how they depend on each other.

Plants produce their own food. They are **producers**.

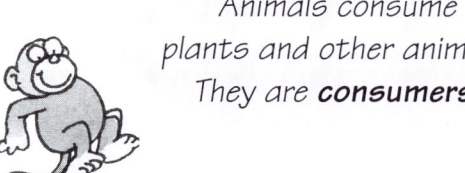

Animals consume plants and other animals. They are **consumers**.

The arrow means 'gives food to'.

producer → 1st consumer → 2nd consumer

These producers and consumers have been put in the wrong order. Write the correct number in the box.

Write 1 in the box if it is a producer. Write 2 if it is the first consumer. Write 3 if it is the second consumer.

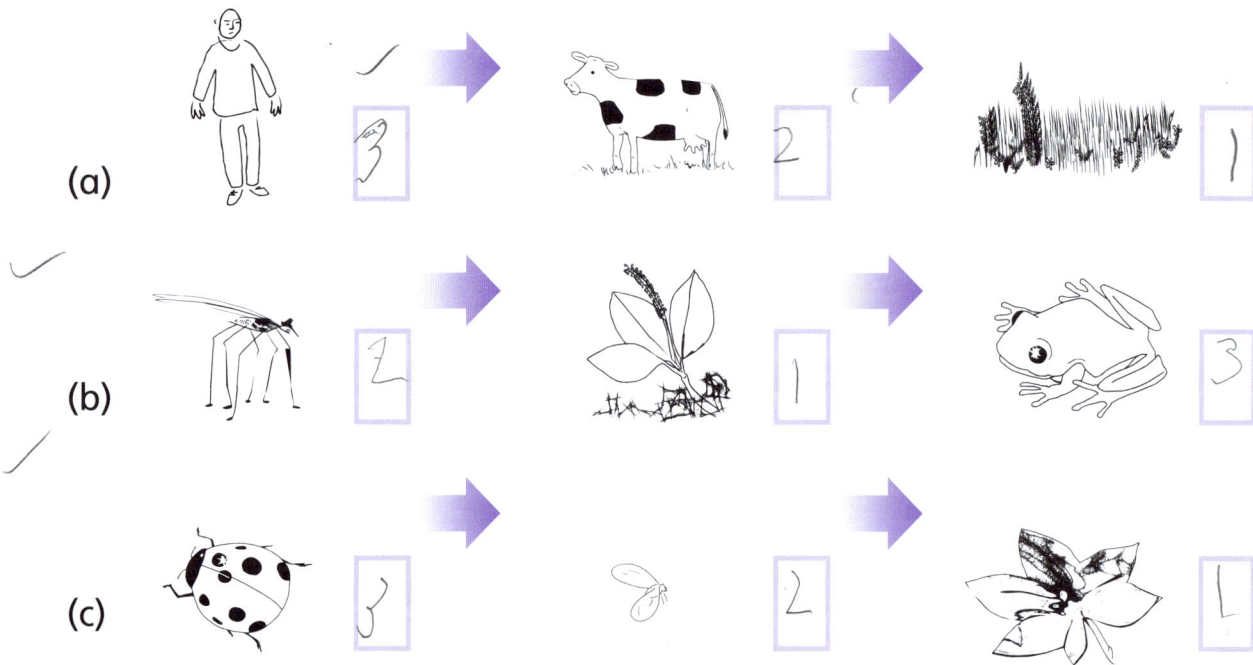

(a) person [3] → cow [2] → grass [1]

(b) dragonfly [2] → plant [1] → frog [3]

(c) ladybug [3] → aphid [2] → flower [1]

2 These food chains are not in the correct order.
Put the correct name in the box next to each arrow.

Which name goes where?

(a) **hedgehog, leaves, slug**

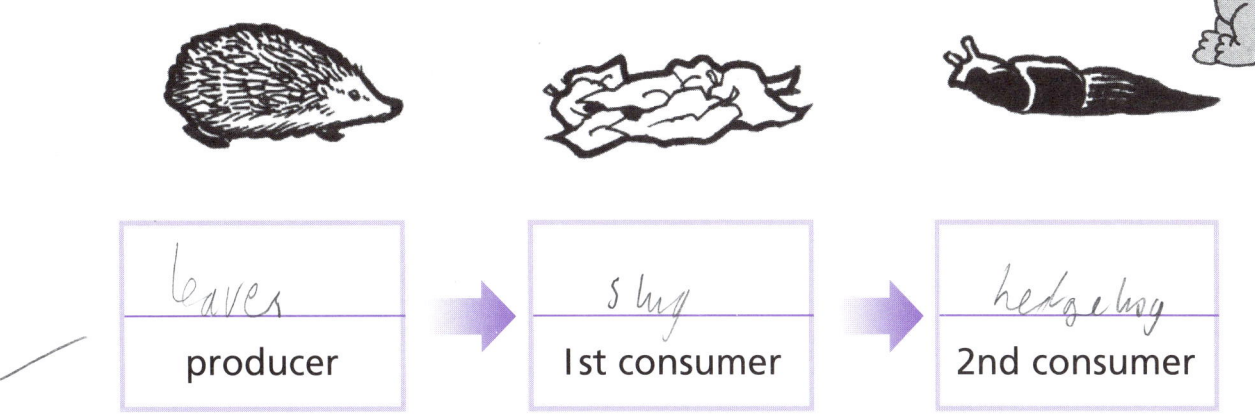

leaves	→	slug	→	hedgehog
producer		1st consumer		2nd consumer

(b) **owl, vole, wheat**

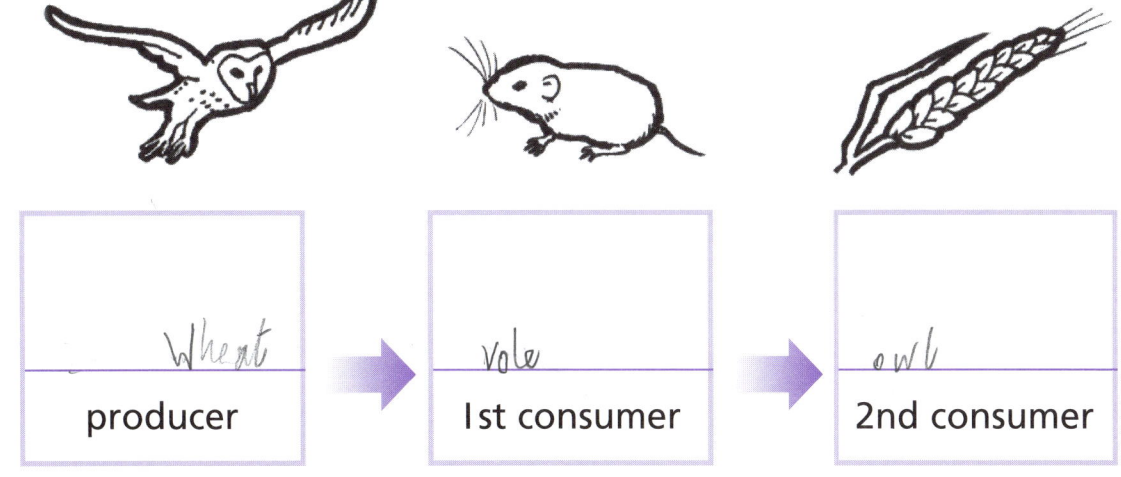

wheat	→	vole	→	owl
producer		1st consumer		2nd consumer

(c) **caterpillar, bluetit, cabbage leaf**

cabbage leaf	→	caterpillar	→	bluetit
producer		1st consumer		2nd consumer

Predator and prey

Here are three food chains.

(a) leaf sap → aphid → ladybird →

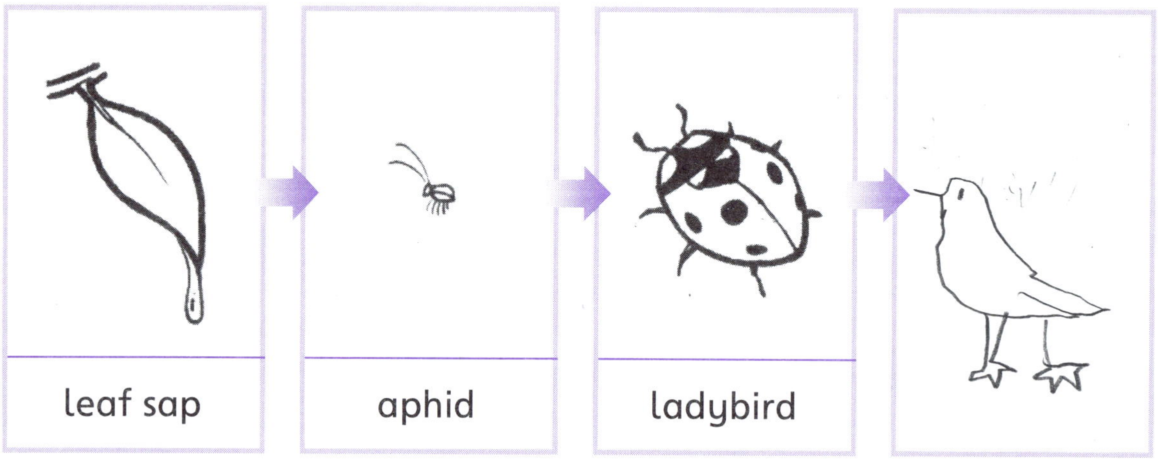

(b) algae → water flea → stickleback →

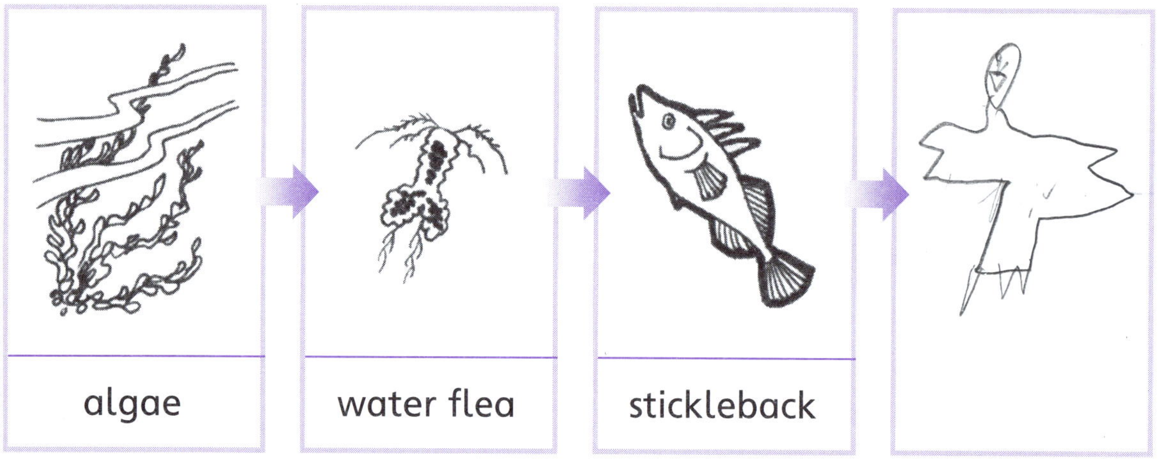

(c) plant remains → earthworm → shrew →

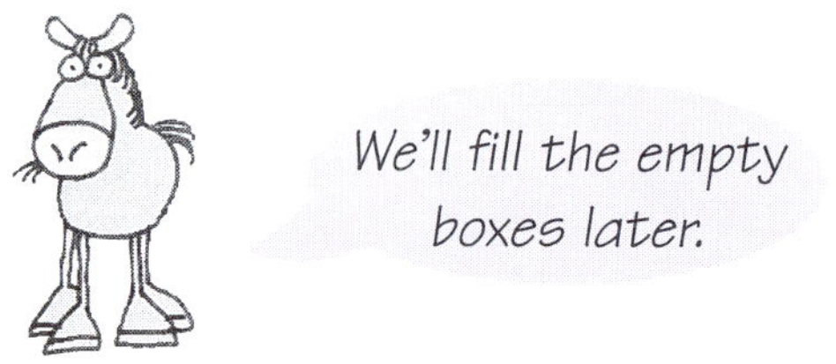

We'll fill the empty boxes later.

16

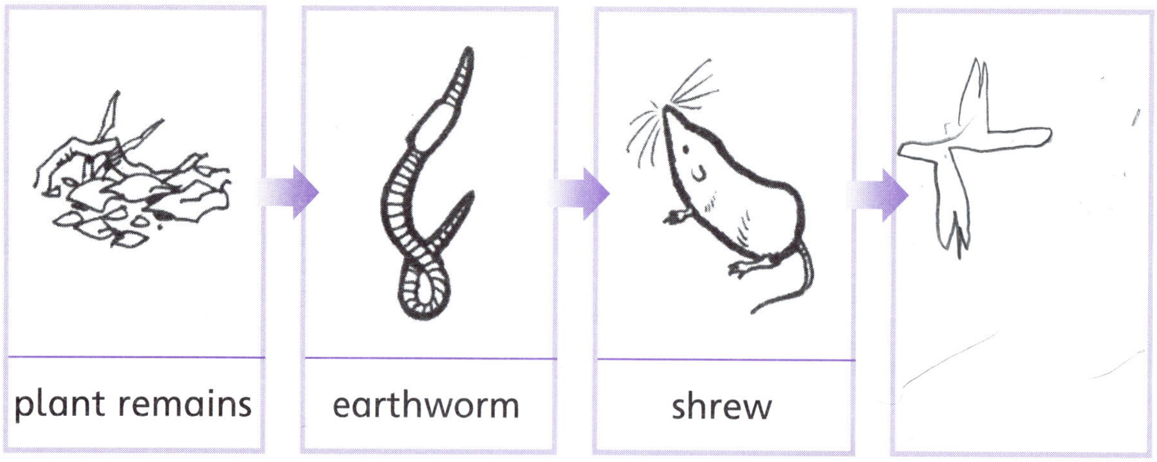

1. Identify the producer, 1st consumer (**prey**) and 2nd consumer (**predator**) in each food chain. Write their names in the table.

Animals which eat other animals are called predators.

Animals which are eaten by other animals are called prey.

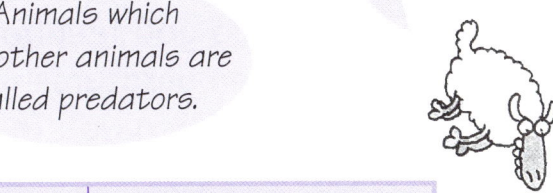

	Producer	1st consumer (prey)	2nd consumer (predator)
(a)	leaf sap	aphid	ladybird
(b)	algae	water flea	stickle back
(c)	plant remains	earthworm	shrew

2. A heron eats sticklebacks, a buzzard eats shrews, a thrush eats ladybirds. Put one of these predators in the correct empty box on the opposite page.

3. What would happen in the first food chain if the number of ladybirds suddenly increased a lot?

   There would be fewer aphids.

Would there be more or fewer aphids?

Would there be more or fewer thrushes?

4. What would happen in the second food chain if the pond was drained?

   The stickleback would die and there will be more water fleas.

What would happen to the algae?

The algae, water fleas and stickleback can only survive in the pond, so if the pond were drained they would all die, without any food the heron would fly away to another pond.

Hot and cold

Temperature is a measure of how hot or cold something is.

1. When do you feel hot or cold? For each of these **temperatures** write a sentence to explain when you feel like this.

   One has been done for you as an example.

   hot   I feel hot when I have been playing football on a summer's day.

   warm   I feel warm when I wear my jumper.

   cool   I feel cool when I go out in the wind.

   cold   I feel cold when it is snowing.

2. To measure temperatures accurately we use a **thermometer**. Put these words in the correct positions on the thermometer.

   cool   (very cold)   warm   cold   hot

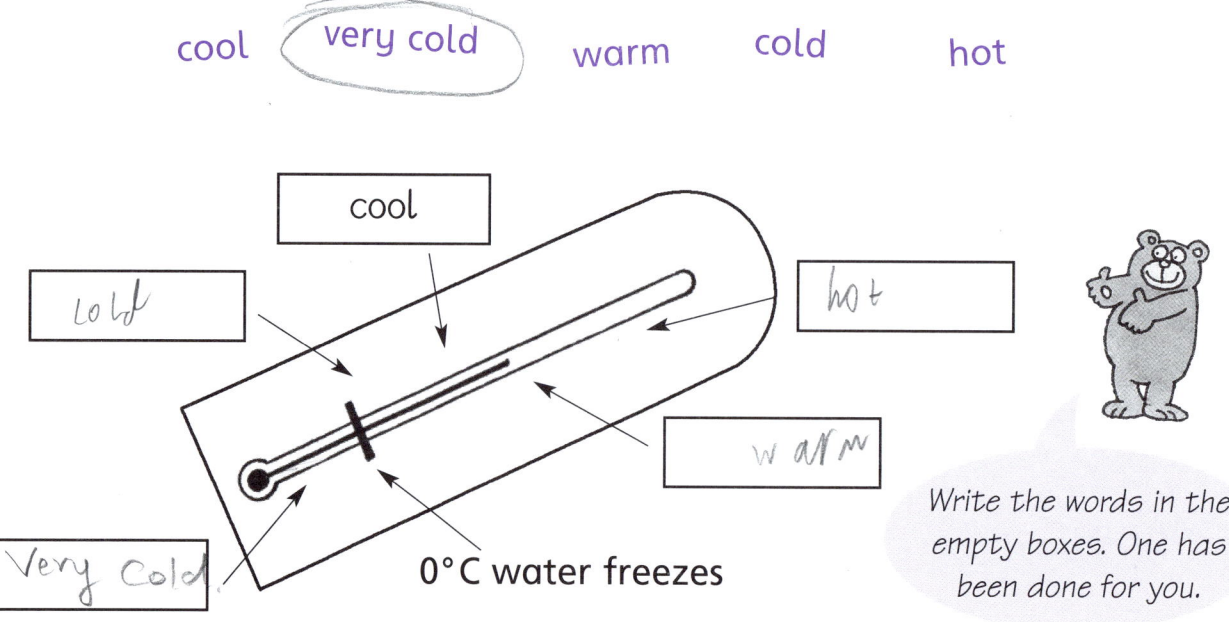

0°C water freezes

Write the words in the empty boxes. One has been done for you.

3 What is the temperature on each of these thermometers? Write your answers in the boxes.

Temperature is measured in small units called degrees Celsius.

We write degrees Celsius °C.

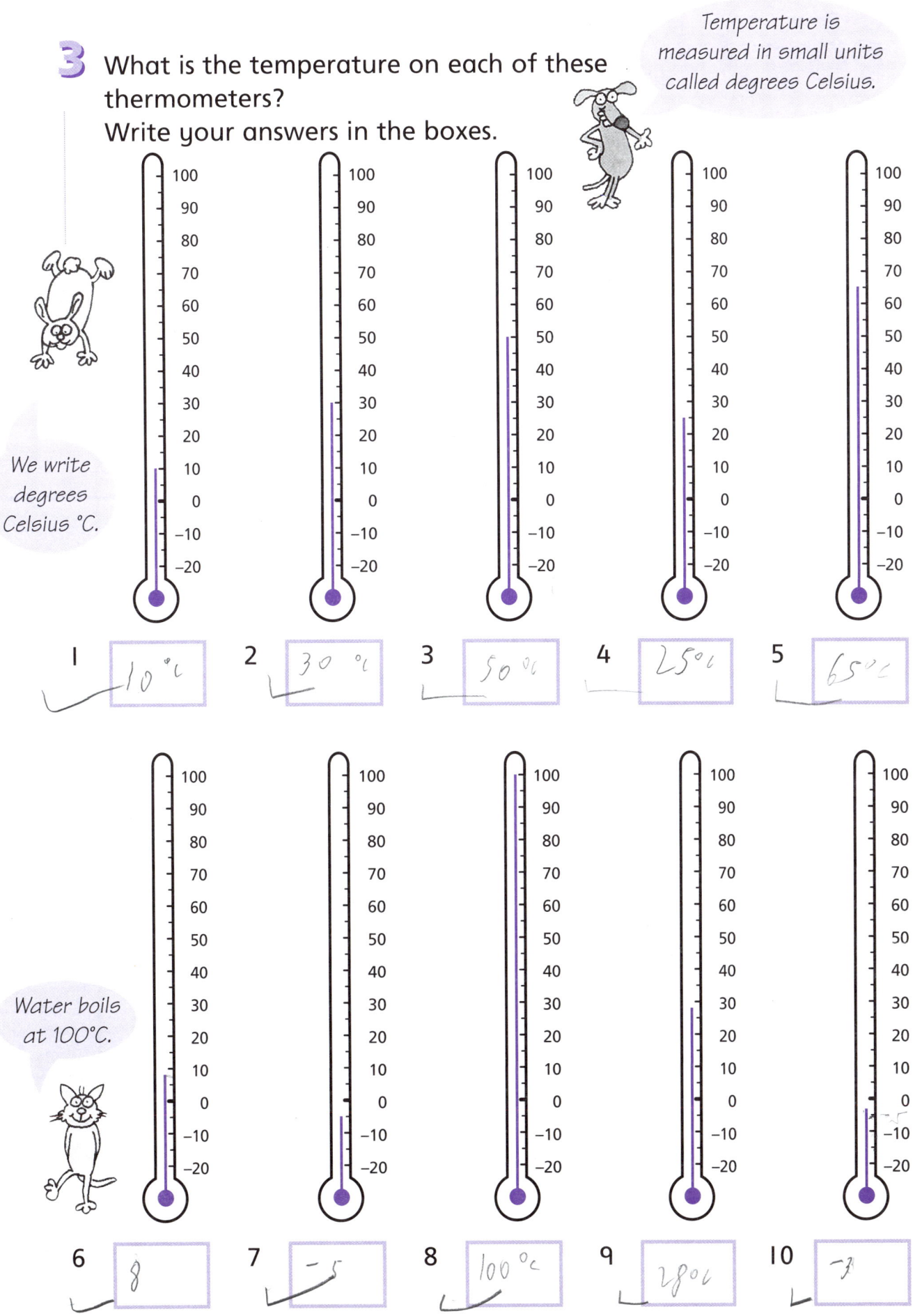

1. 10 °C
2. 30 °C
3. 50 °C
4. 25 °C
5. 65 °C

Water boils at 100°C.

6. 8
7. −5
8. 100 °C
9. 28 °C
10. −7

The right temperature

1. These pictures show different **temperatures**. Find the right temperature to match the picture and fill in the thermometer correctly.

   -3°C   25°C   100°C   −10°C

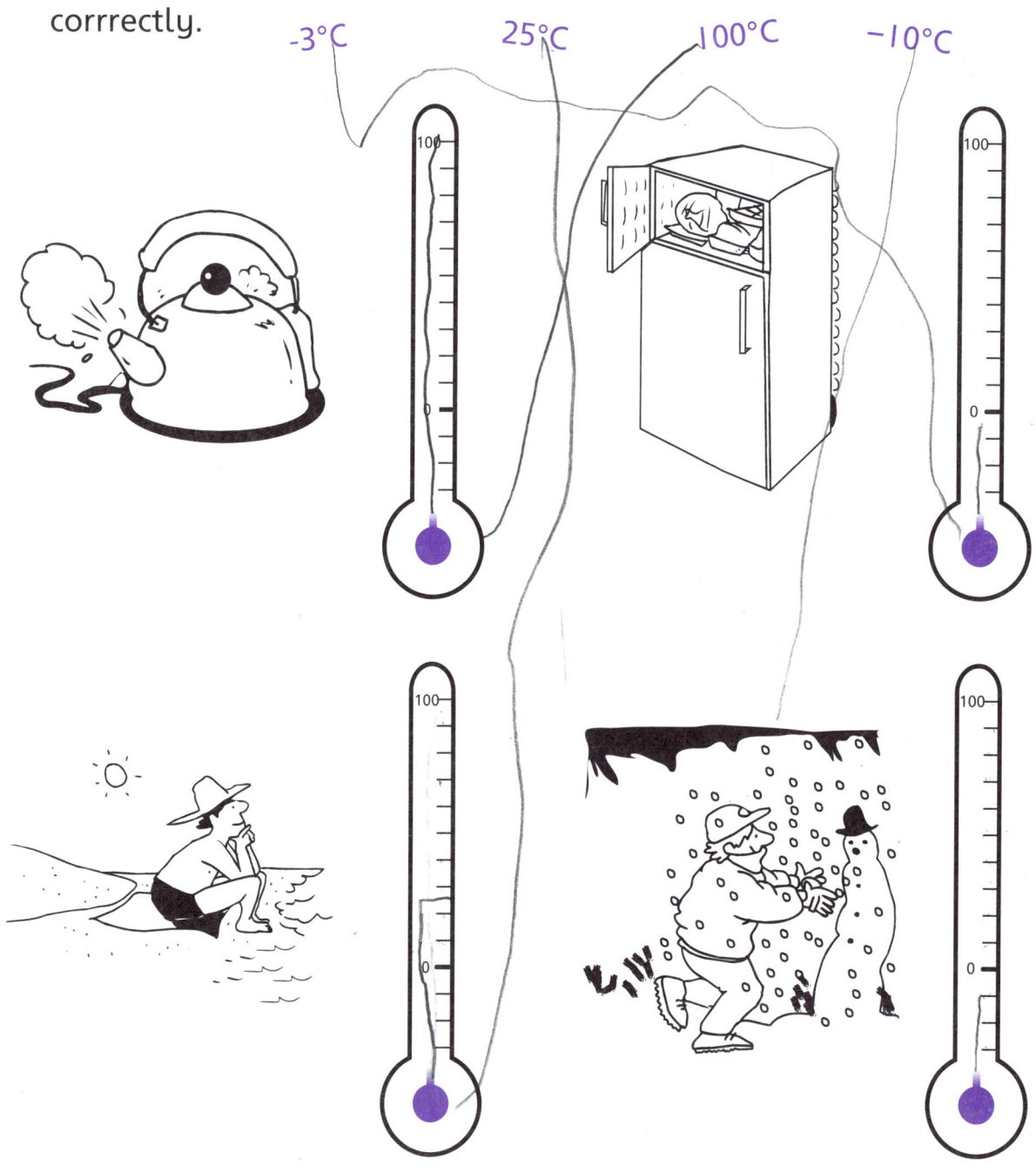

2. Put the temperatures in order starting with the coldest.

   __−10°C__   __−3°C__   __25°C__   __100°C__
   coldest   hottest

Room temperature

My dinner is getting cold.

Look what's happened to my ice-cream!

Emily and Ian want to find out whether the temperature of solids and liquids rises or falls to match the surrounding air. They test this by leaving a jar of hot water where the temperature is 25° Celsius. They read and record the temperature every 10 minutes.

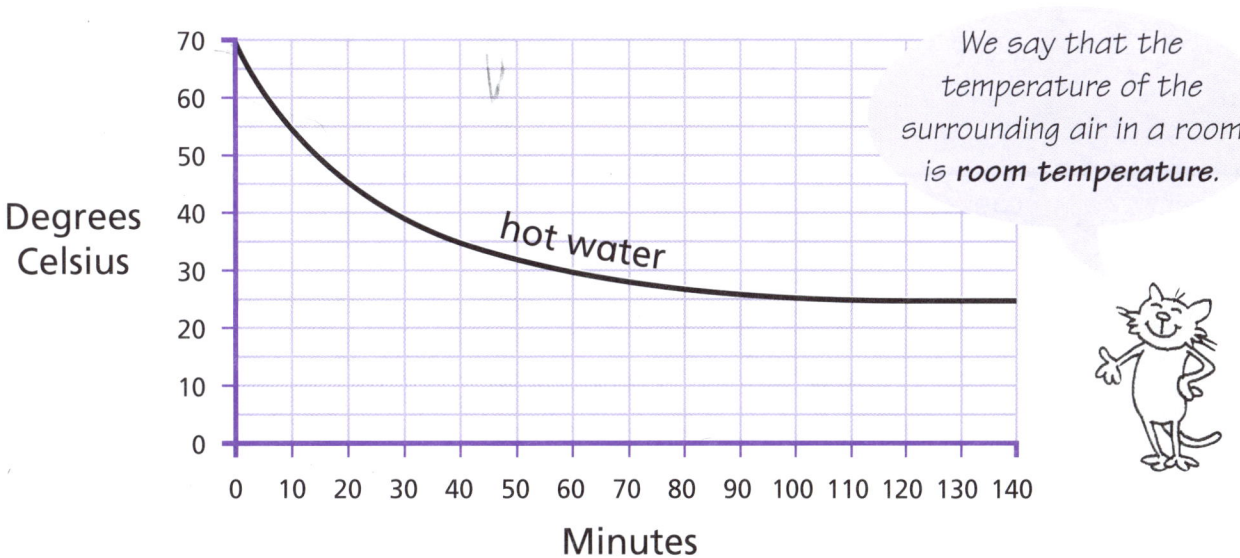

*We say that the temperature of the surrounding air in a room is **room temperature**.*

1. Look carefully at the graph. What has happened to the temperature of the water?

   The water has got colder.

2. Why do you think this happened?

   _____

3. How long did it take for the water to reach room temperature?

   _____

4. What would happen to ice cubes if they were left out in this room?

   They would melt.

   Why? _Because it would and the would into water_

21

Home hot spots

Here is a plan of a kitchen. Some areas are hot, others are cold.

1 Mark the warm or hot places in red.

2 Mark the cool or cold places in blue.

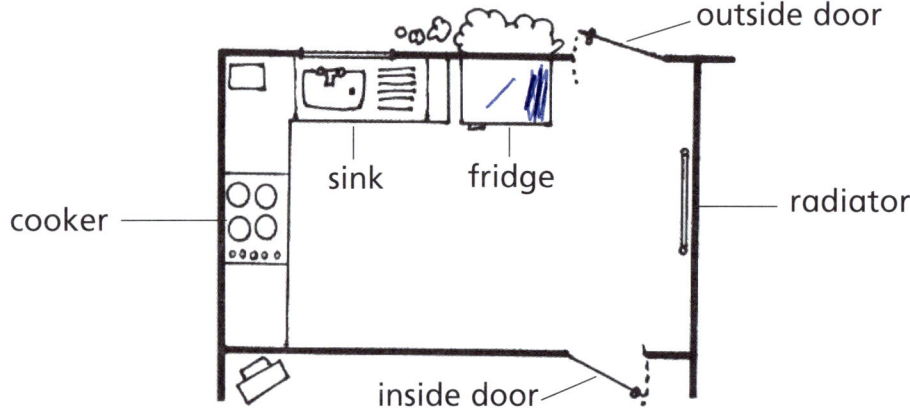

3 Draw a plan of a room in your house. Mark on the hot and cold places in the same way.

Stay cool

We want our drinks to stay cool.

Anna and Wesley tested which materials would keep their drinks cold.

They measured the temperature every 10 minutes in degrees Celsius.

Here are their results.

> We call materials that keep things cold **insulators**.

Readings	1st	2nd	3rd	4th	5th	6th
No insulation	5	9	12	15	17	18
Wool	5	7	9	10	11	12
Felt	5	8	11	13	14	16
Cotton	5	9	12	14	16	17
Bubble wrap	5	8	10	12	13	14

1 Look carefully at the results.
What has happened to the temperature for each material?

_____

2 Put the four materials in order starting with the material which was best at keeping the drinks cool.

~~No insulation~~ cotton _____ felt _____ No insulation
Wool

3 What do you think Anna and Wesley did to make sure that their test was fair?

thay hot water in any of them

> In a fair test only one thing is changed each time.

Thermal insulators

Insulators are materials which keep cold objects cold and warm objects warm.

We call these **thermal** insulators.

1. Draw a picture of some of the clothes you would wear in winter.

Air is a good insulator. Some materials trap a layer of air.

Metals are not good thermal insulators because they let heat pass through or move along them.

We say metals **conduct** heat.

2. What materials are these clothes made from? Why?

_____

3. Why do you think saucepans have wooden or plastic handles?

_____

4. In this picture there are lots of thermal insulators. Colour them red.

Temperature search

1 There are 11 words in this **temperature** search. How many can you find? Colour the words or draw a ring around them.

n	j	c	e	l	s	i	u	s	r
q	t	l	h	f	l	n	a	p	t
d	e	g	r	e	e	s	e	i	h
t	m	b	p	r	a	u	u	x	e
l	p	u	c	o	o	l	b	l	r
a	e	g	m	i	q	a	o	g	m
i	r	d	p	h	o	t	i	a	o
w	a	r	m	v	l	e	l	v	m
k	t	l	e	k	d	s	o	j	e
c	u	m	c	o	n	d	u	c	t
s	r	t	z	f	h	s	y	i	e
a	e	f	r	e	e	z	e	o	r

insulate   Celsius

degrees   temperature

hot   cool   warm

thermometer   conduct

boil   freeze

These are the words you are looking for. They all have something to do with temprature.

The words read across from left to right or downwards.

Write your ✓ or ✗ in the boxes.

2 **True or false?**

Put a ✓ next to the statements that you think are correct.
Put a ✗ next to the statements that you think are wrong.

(a) Temperature is a measure of how hot or cold something is.

(b) Metals are not good thermal conductors.

(c) The reading on a thermometer goes down if it is hot.

(d) We use a temperature to measure thermometers.

(e) A thermal insulator keeps cold objects cold.

(f) Plastics and wood are not good thermal insulators but metals are.

25

Danger — electricity!

Electricity can be very **dangerous** if it is not used properly.

1 Look at this picture. Draw a ring around the dangers.

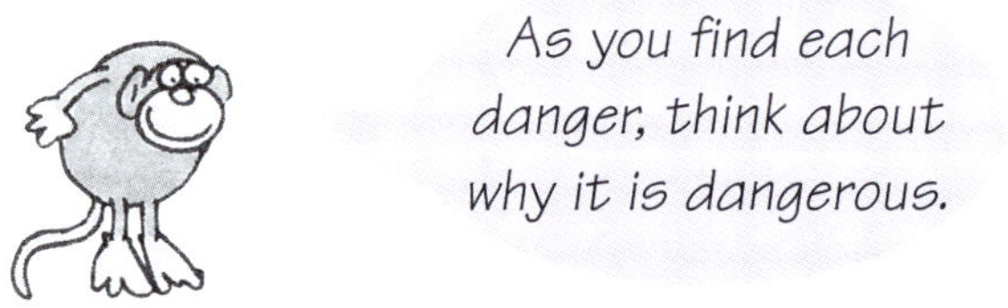

As you find each danger, think about why it is dangerous.

2 How many dangers did you find? _____

Safety first

Complete this puzzle by answering the clues.

We must be very careful with electricity.

Write the answers to the clues in the correct boxes.

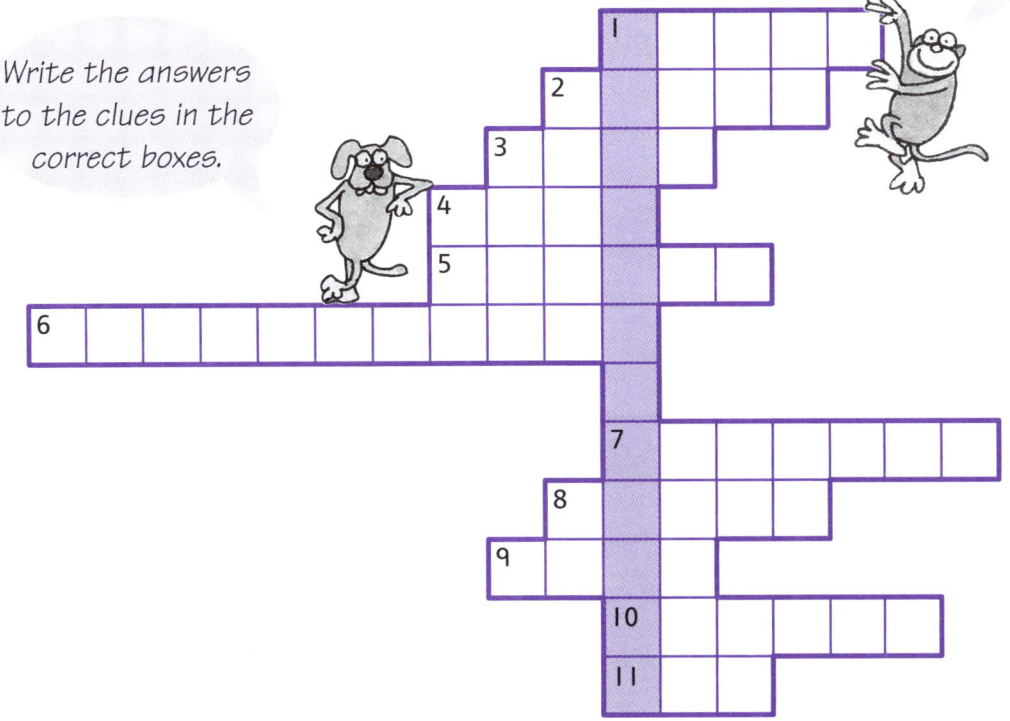

Clues (all across)

1. If you play with electricity, you may get one of these!
2. Never splash this onto an electric socket.
3. Better this than sorry!
4. Electricity flows through this to an appliance.
5. Use this to turn the lights on or off.
6. Think safety whenever you use this.
7. Don't stick your _____ in the sockets in the wall.
8. An electric bulb gives you this when it is turned on.
9. _____ on the switch!
10. What a plug is pushed into.
11. _____ many plugs connected to a socket is dangerous.

What message is spelled out in the shaded squares of the puzzle?

_____ _____

Going round

The path that electricity flows round is called a **circuit**.

The circuit must be **complete** to allow the electricity to flow.

In a complete circuit the wires are connected correctly to the battery and to the bulb holder ...

... and the light bulb is screwed in.

1 Look carefully at each circuit to see if it is complete. If it is then colour in the light bulb yellow.

2 Underneath each picture explain why the bulb does light or doesn't light.

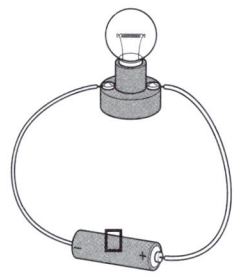   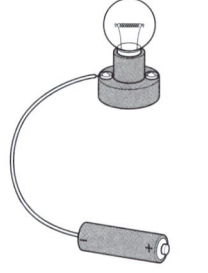   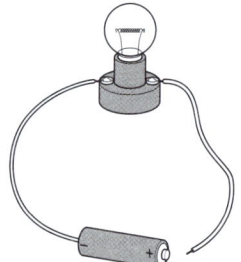

(a) _____   (b) _____   (c) _____

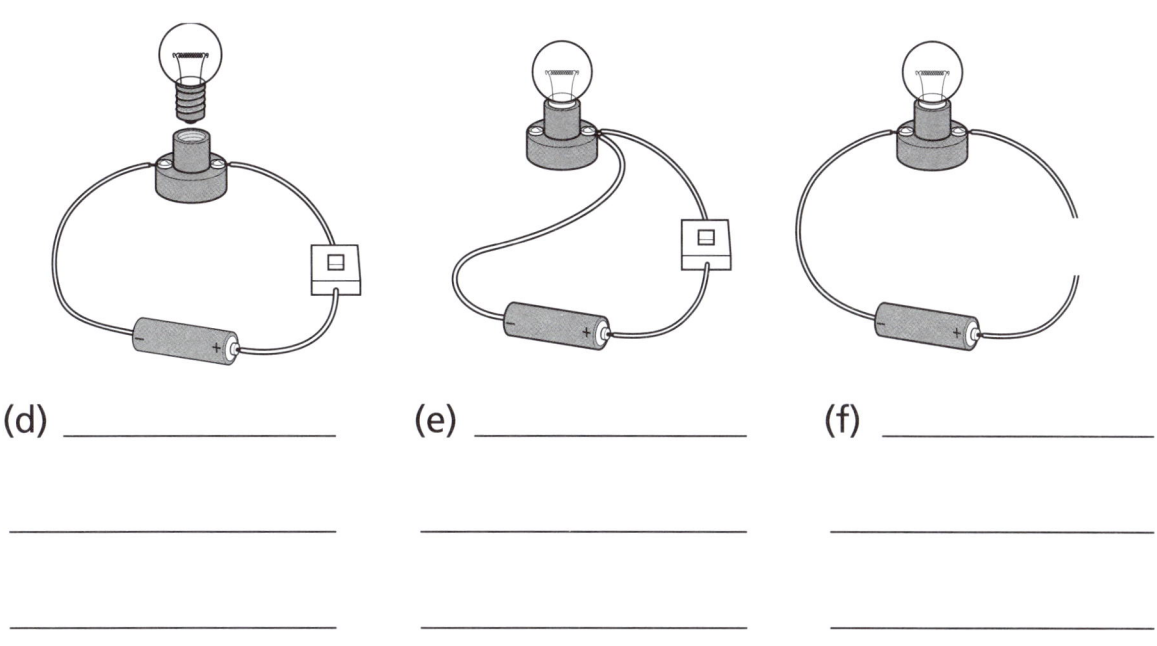

(d) _____ (e) _____ (f) _____

_____   _____   _____

_____   _____   _____

A switch is a break in the circuit. This is one way we can control the flow of the electricity around the circuit.

If the switch is on, the circuit is complete.

If the switch is off, the circuit is broken.

3 Look at these pictures. Is the switch on or off? Write On or Off underneath each picture.

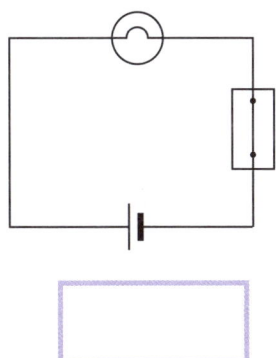 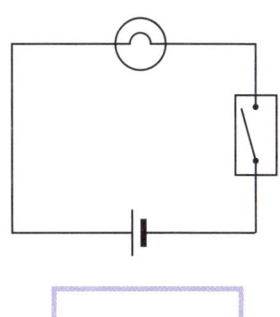 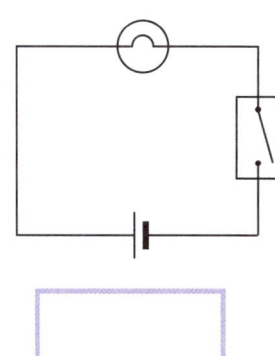

4 List six objects which have a switch.

_____   _____   _____

_____   _____   _____

29

To conduct or not ...

Materials that allow electricity to pass through are called **electrical conductors**.

Sanjay made a circuit like this one.

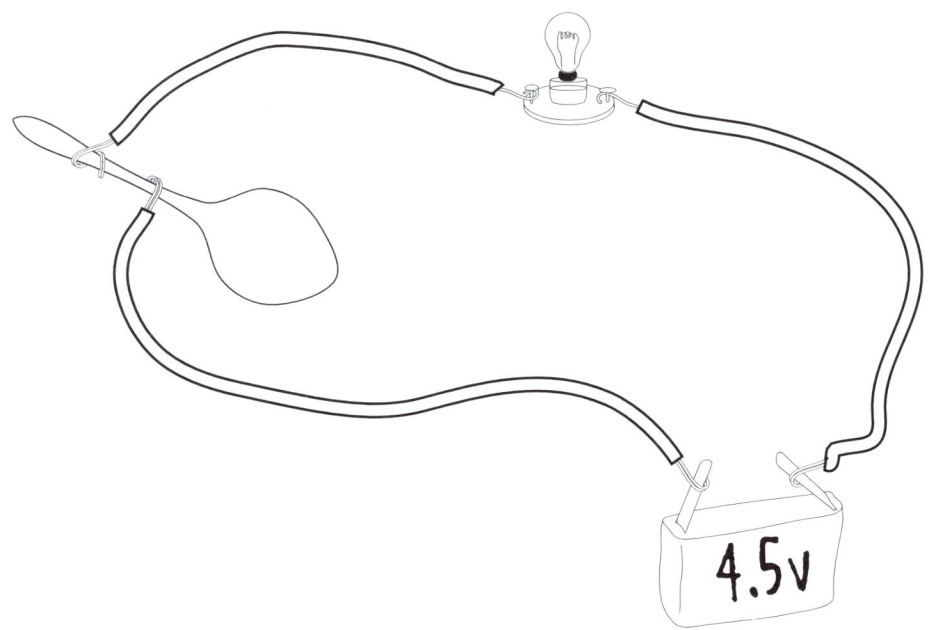

Sara gathered together these items to make similar circuits.

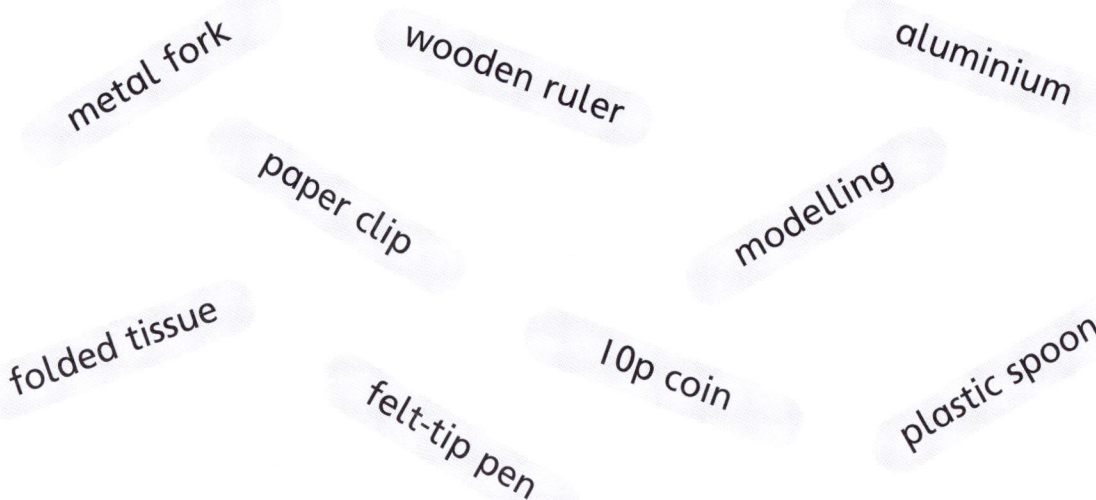

metal fork, wooden ruler, aluminium, paper clip, modelling, folded tissue, felt-tip pen, 10p coin, plastic spoon

1. Which of the items will conduct electricity so that the bulb will light?

   _____   _____   _____   _____

2. What is similar about the items you have listed?

   _____

   _____

What are the items that conduct electricity made from?

3. What other items do you think would conduct electricity?

   _____

   _____

4. Can you spot four things wrong in this picture? Draw a ring around them.

What things would you change so that everything will work?

Will all the electrical items work?

Electrical insulators

Materials that do not allow electricity to pass through are called **electrical insulators**.

In a circuit some of the materials used are conductors and some are insulators.

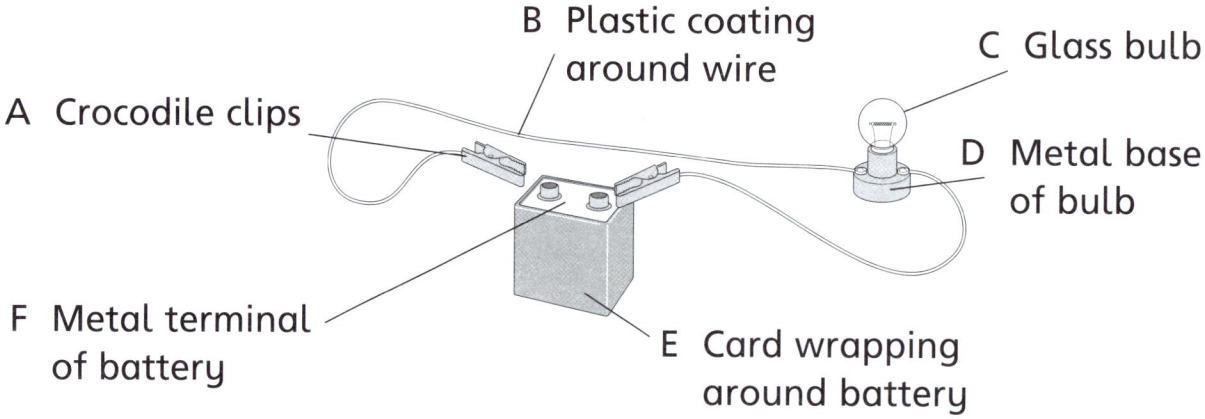

A Crocodile clips
B Plastic coating around wire
C Glass bulb
D Metal base of bulb
E Card wrapping around battery
F Metal terminal of battery

1 Write down the parts which are insulators and the parts which are conductors.

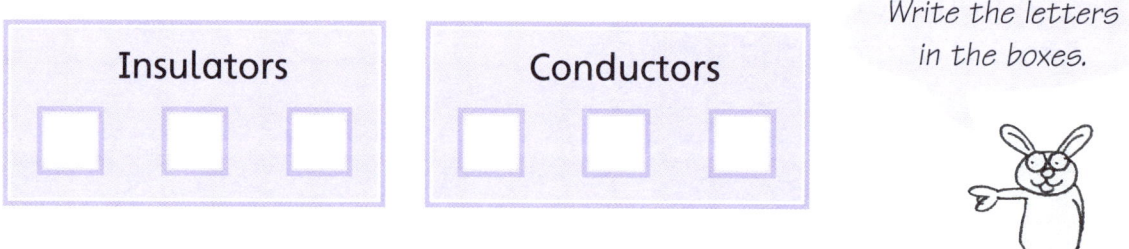

Insulators ☐ ☐ ☐

Conductors ☐ ☐ ☐

Write the letters in the boxes.

2 Electrical plugs also have parts made from insulators and conductors. Explain why each part is an insulator or conductor.

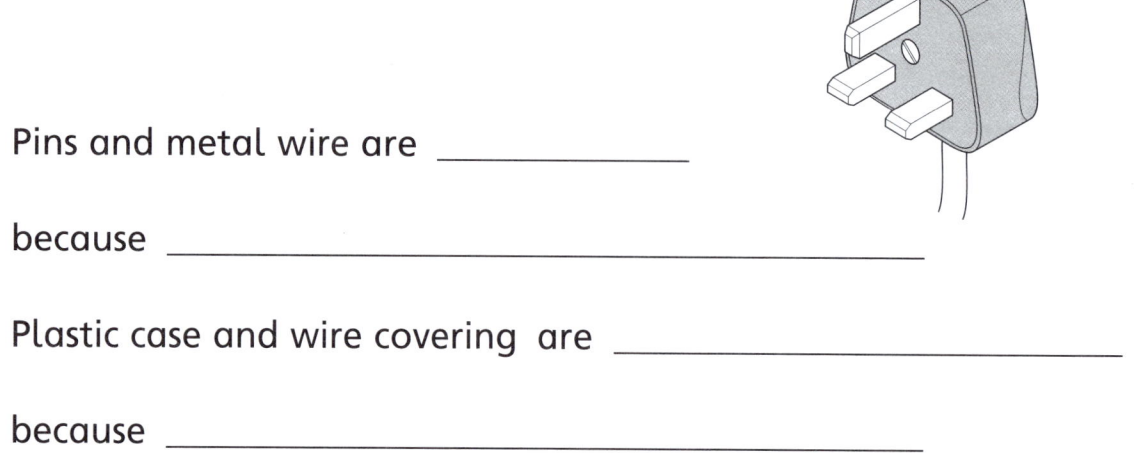

Pins and metal wire are _____

because _____

Plastic case and wire covering are _____

because _____

Sort it

Many items require either a **battery** or **mains electricity** to work.

If it's plugged into electric sockets it uses mains electricity.

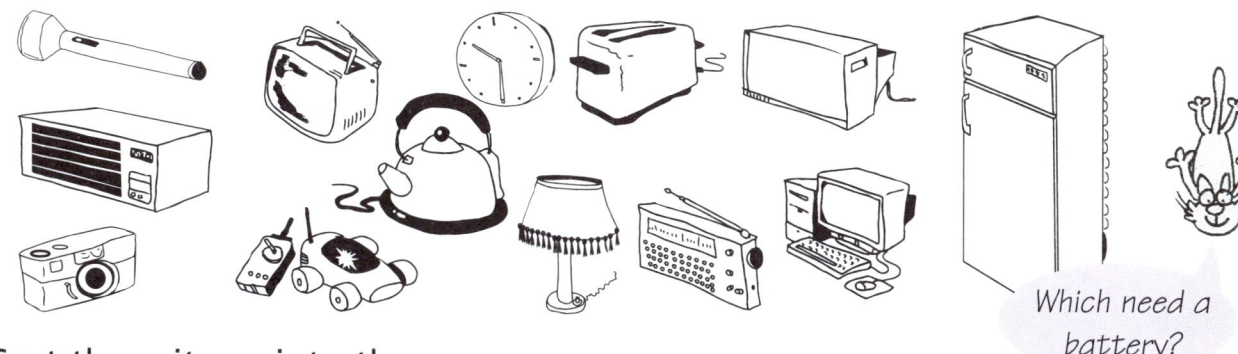

1 Sort these items into three groups:

- Those operated by battery.
- Those operated by mains electricity.
- Those which can be operated by both.

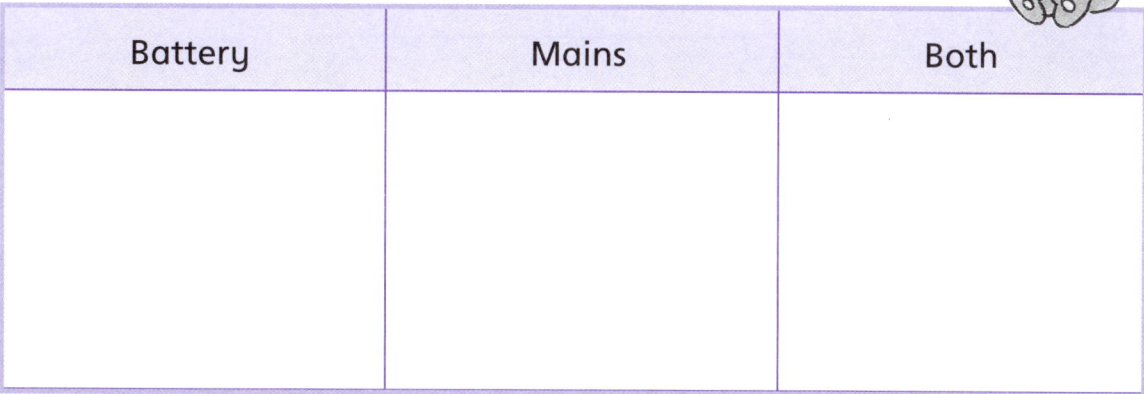

Which need a battery?

Which need mains electricity?

Battery	Mains	Both

2 Why don't the mains operated items use batteries?

_____

_____

3 Why don't the battery operated items use mains electricity?

_____

_____

On the move

All these animals **move** in different ways.

1. Write the names of these animals in their correct positions on the **sorting tree**.

   deer wallaby gull fish snake monkey

   Does this animal fly?
   - Yes → (a)
   - No → Does it spend all its life swimming in water?
     - Yes → (b)
     - No → Does it move about on legs?
       - Yes → Does it climb trees?
         - Yes → (d)
         - No → Does it move on two legs?
           - Yes → (e)
           - No → (f)
       - No → (c)

2. Which box do humans belong to on the sorting tree? ☐

Them bones

Your **skeleton** is made up from lots of **bones** joined together.

1. Label the bones on this skeleton.

      skull   rib   knee cap   collar bone   jaw

      spine (back bone)   shoulder blade   thigh bone

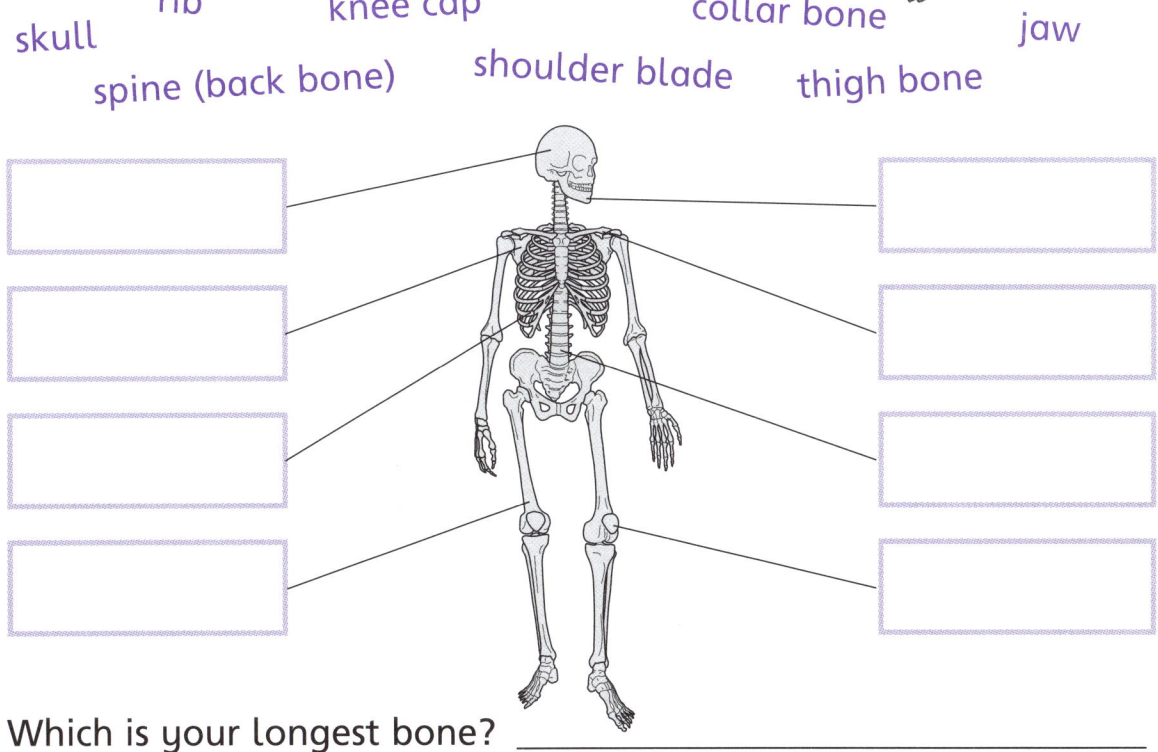

2. Which is your longest bone? _____

3. Do you know the names of any other bones? Label them on the skeleton.

Your bones keep important parts of your body safe.

4. Which bones protect these important parts? Look at the picture to help you.

    (a) heart   _____

    (b) spinal cord   _____

    (c) brain   _____

Did you know there are 206 bones in your body?

X-rays

Doctors use X-ray photos to see if a bone is broken.

X-ray photos show us what our bones look like.

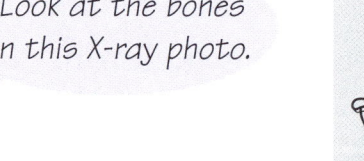

Look at the bones in this X-ray photo.

1 Underline the words which describe what bones are like.

heavy   hard   bendy   soft   light   weak

rough   uneven   jagged   sharp   strong   smooth

2 These are skeletons of some animals. Which skeleton is which?

| fish |
| bird |
| snake |
| cat |
| frog |

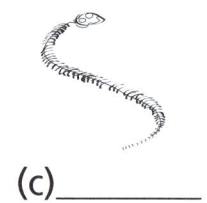

(a)_____

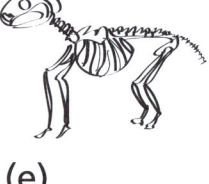

(c)_____

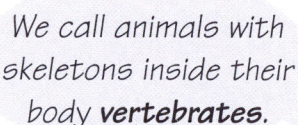

Write the name of the animal underneath the correct skeleton.

(b)_____   (d)_____

(e)_____

3 What do all these skeletons have in common.

We call animals with skeletons inside their body **vertebrates**.

_____

_____

4 Draw what you think a cat's broken leg bone would look like in an X-ray.

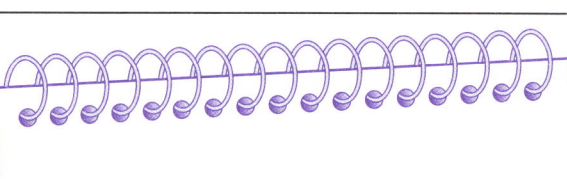

36

Muscles

Animals with skeletons have **muscles** attached to the bones. These muscles help the bones to move.

Think about how you move your whole body and how you move parts of your body. One has been done for you.

1 In how many different ways can you move your body?

jump _____ _____ _____ _____

_____ _____ _____ _____ _____

Look what happens to Tom when he has a race. Lots of his **muscles** have to work hard in order to move his body quickly.

Try to think of at least four different words.

2 Write down how you think Tom feels at the end of the race.

_____ _____ _____ _____

3 (a) What has happened to Tom's muscles?

_____

(b) How has his breathing changed? _____

(c) How has his heartbeat changed? _____

37

*These animals are all **invertebrates**.*

Body support

Not all animals have skeletons inside them. Animals which do not have internal skeletons are called **invertebrates**.

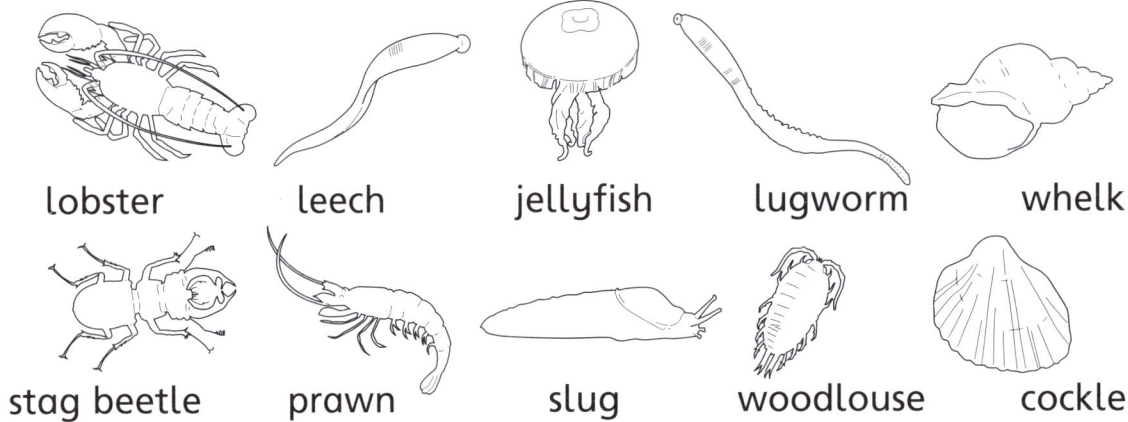

lobster   leech   jellyfish   lugworm   whelk

stag beetle   prawn   slug   woodlouse   cockle

1 Some of these invertebrates wear their skeletons on the outside like a suit of armour. Colour them **red**.

2 Others have no skeleton. Colour them **blue**.

3 In this word search there are 14 **invertebrates**. Draw a ring around them when you find them.

Words read across from left to right or downwards.

These are the invertebrates you are looking for.

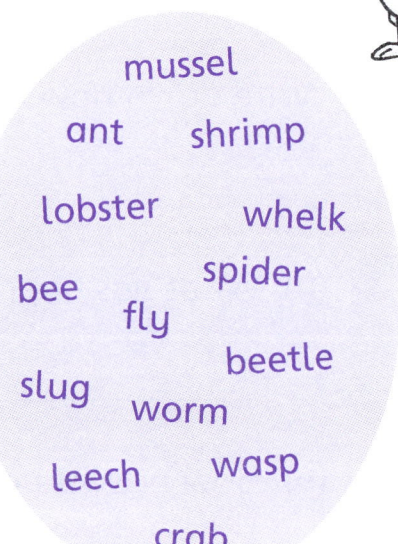

s	h	r	i	m	p	v	i	d	o	s
b	u	a	s	i	w	c	w	a	s	p
k	l	f	l	y	e	s	m	e	h	i
c	d	r	a	s	w	a	c	a	u	d
r	k	b	c	g	w	o	y	n	o	e
a	l	e	f	l	o	b	s	t	e	r
b	e	e	h	s	r	t	o	z	i	d
r	e	t	a	w	m	u	s	s	e	l
f	c	l	o	p	x	r	t	l	e	d
w	h	e	l	k	c	h	i	u	b	a
g	r	u	y	b	u	b	u	g	e	n

mussel   ant   shrimp   lobster   whelk   bee   spider   fly   slug   beetle   worm   leech   wasp   crab

Creepy crawlies

Some **invertebrates** have hard outer skeletons or shells. These are used to give protection and provide support for the animal. Muscles are attached on the inside of the skeleton to enable the animal to move.

Now colour in the pictures in the boxes.

Match the boxes to the correct information.

Draw lines to match the boxes.

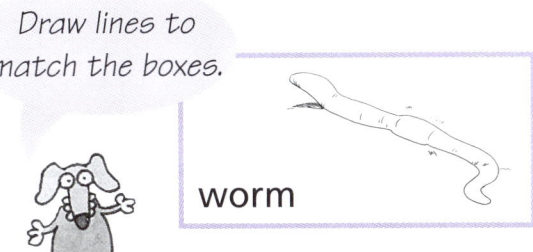
worm

Has a coiled shell to protect the soft body. It moves by gliding along on its muscular foot, taking its shell with it.

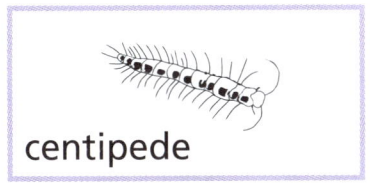
centipede

Has no skeleton and no legs. It moves by using its muscles to make its body long and thin and then short and fat.

ladybird

Has a jointed outer skeleton which enables the animal to roll up into a ball. It has 14 legs.

crab

Has a hard, outer skeleton and about 30 legs. When it grows, the old skin splits and the animal comes out with a new larger skin.

woodlouse

Has an outer skeleton including a set of hard, red wing cases which protect the thin wings used for flight.

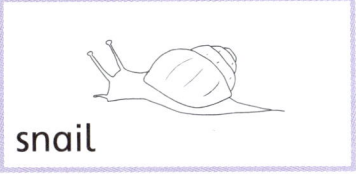
snail

Has a very hard outer skeleton with jointed legs so it can move easily under the water and on land.

Pushes and pulls

Look carefully at each of these pictures.

1. Underneath each picture write whether it shows a **push**, a **pull** or a **twist**.

2. Draw an arrow on each picture to show the direction of the push, pull or twist.

(a)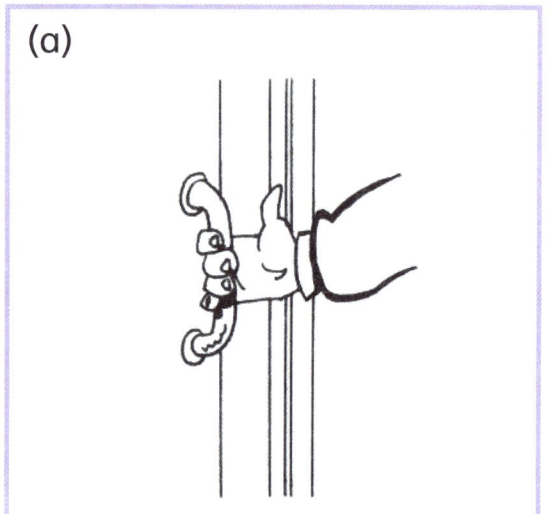

_____

(b)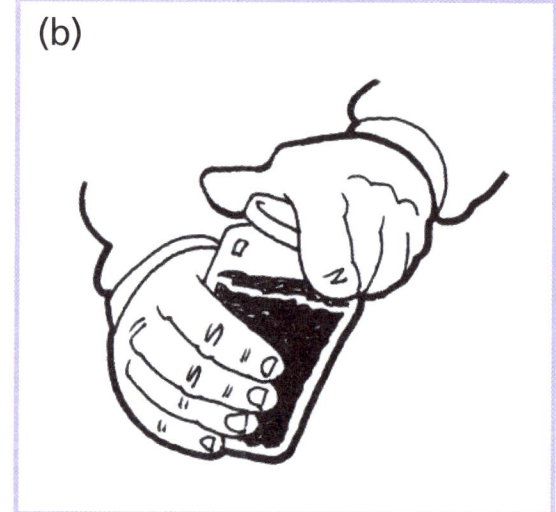

_____

(c)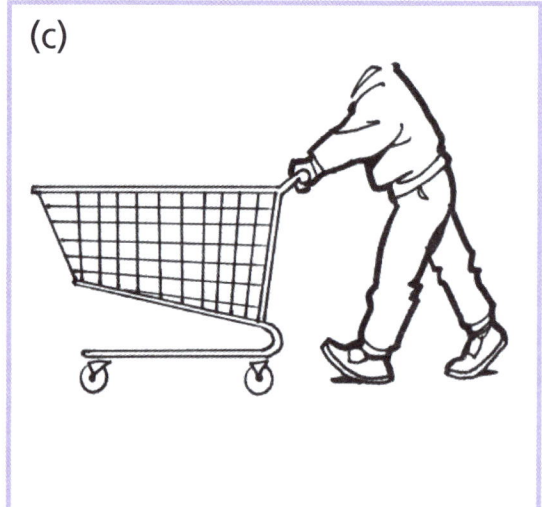

_____

(d)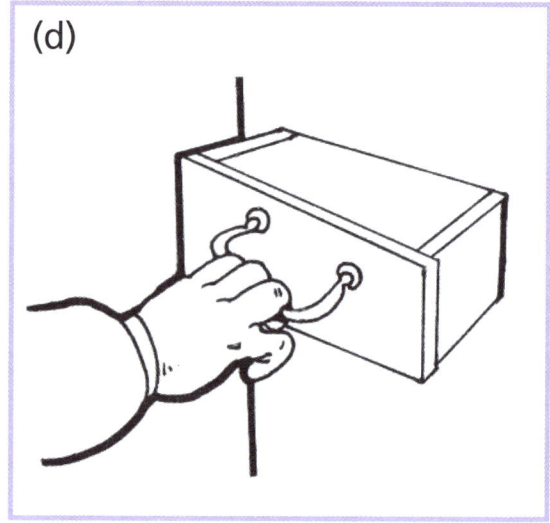

_____

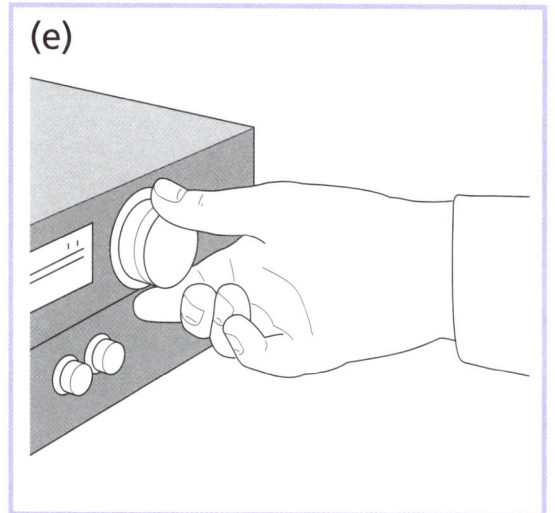 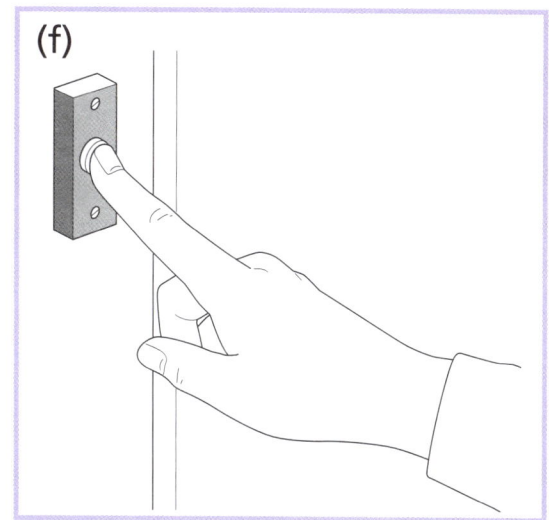

_____   _____

 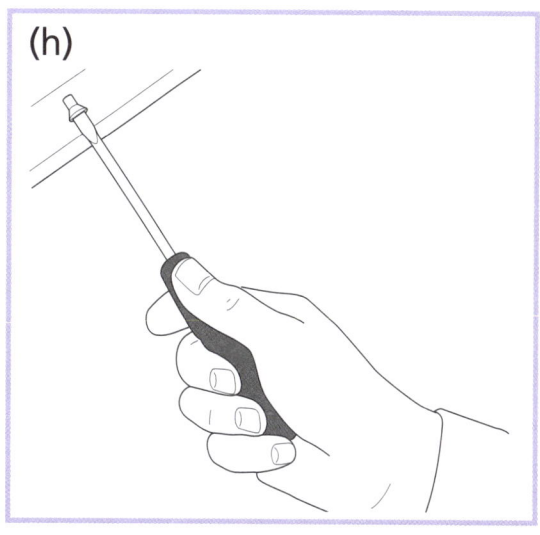

_____   _____

3 Think of more pushes, pulls and twists. Write an example of each in the table.

What do you do when you put on your shoes?

Do you push your feet into them or pull the shoes on?

Push	
Pull	
Twist	

41

It's a drag!

Nina and Robert wanted to test how easily objects **slide** on different surfaces. They collected these items:

- an empty ice-cream tub
- a bag of sugar
- a large elastic band
- a piece of string 60 cm long
- a ruler

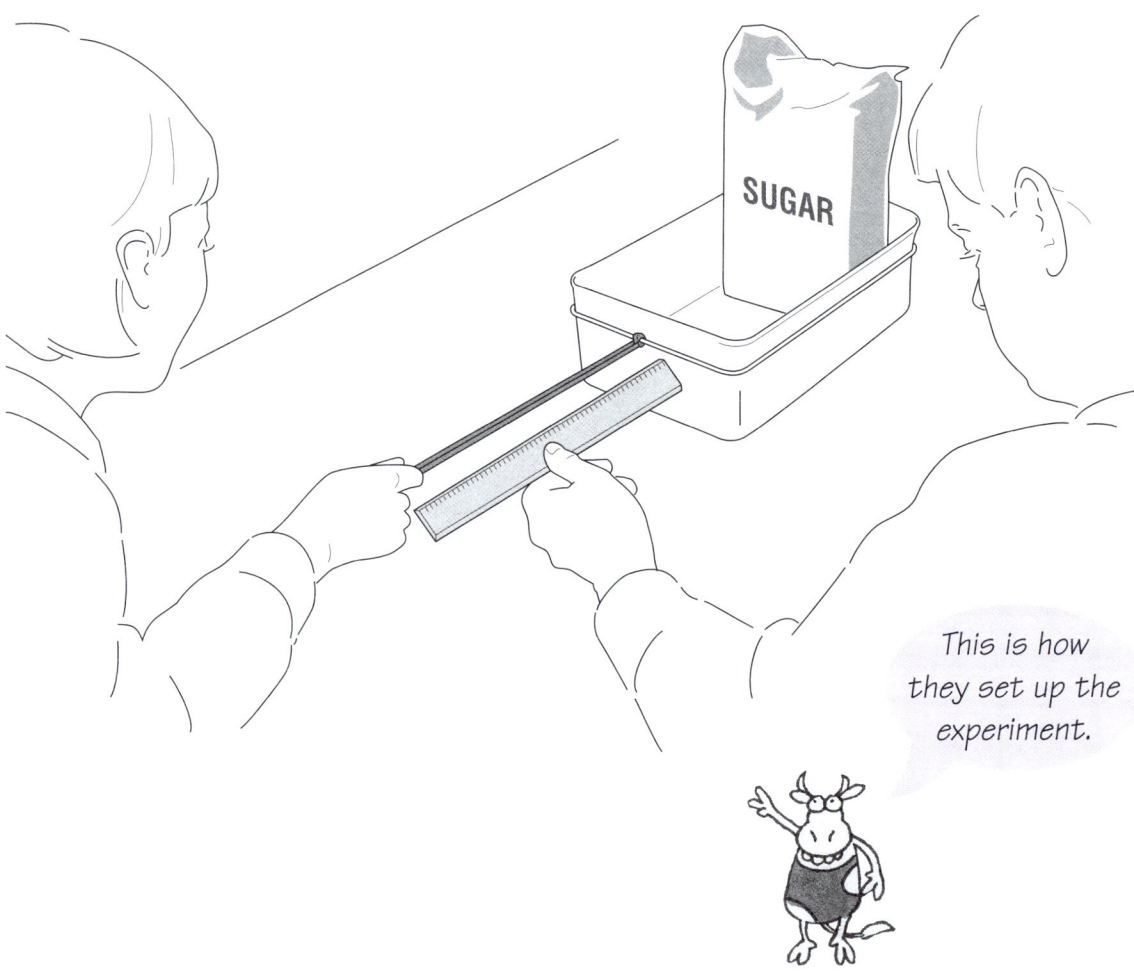

This is how they set up the experiment.

Nina pulled the end of the elastic band and Robert measured how far the band was stretched when the box started to move. They repeated the test four times on each of three different surfaces: carpet, vinyl and wood.

Which surface do you think will be best for sliding?

These are the measurements they recorded.

Surface	Measurement (cm)			
	1st test	2nd test	3rd test	4th test
carpet	14	12	12	13
vinyl	10	10	9	10
wood	9	8	9	9

1 Draw a **bar chart** to show the measurements.

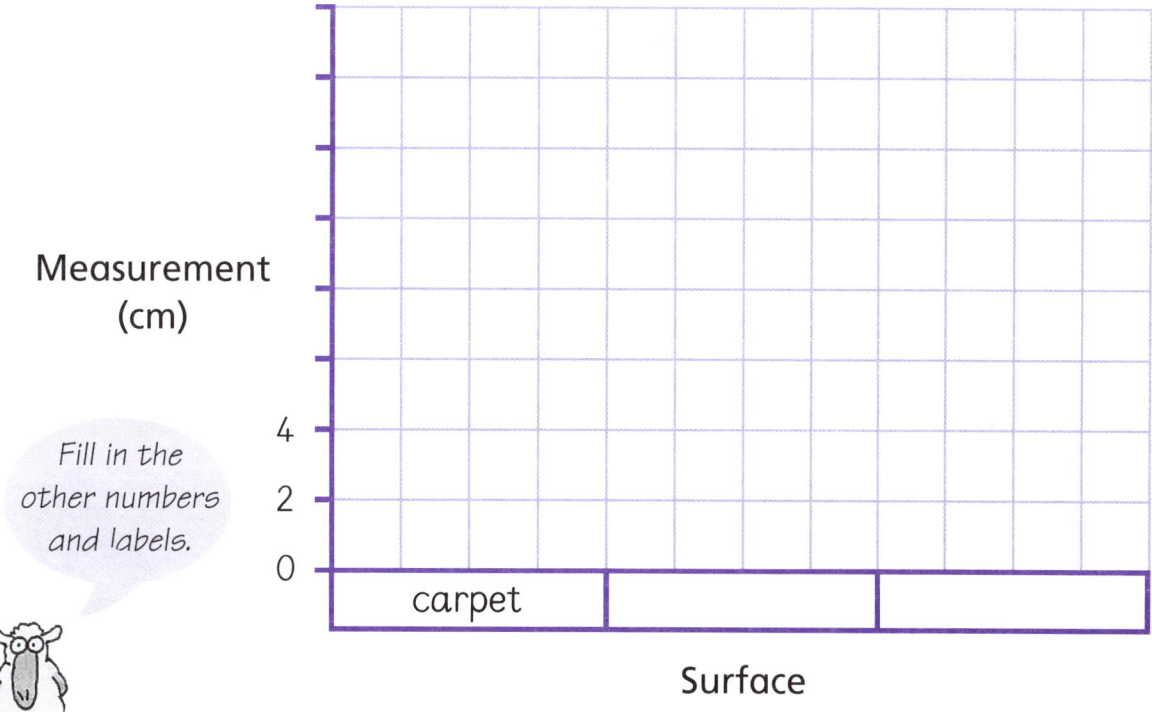

Fill in the other numbers and labels.

2 On which surface did the ice-cream tub slide most easily?

_____

3 Why did Nina and Robert need to repeat the test?

_____

43

Useful friction

Friction is the **force** which slows moving objects down where their two surfaces meet.

Sometimes it is useful to have a lot of friction. At other times, you don't want any friction.

High friction is when there is a lot of friction between two surfaces.

Low friction is when there is very little or no friction.

1. Label each picture as **high friction** or **low friction**.

(a) 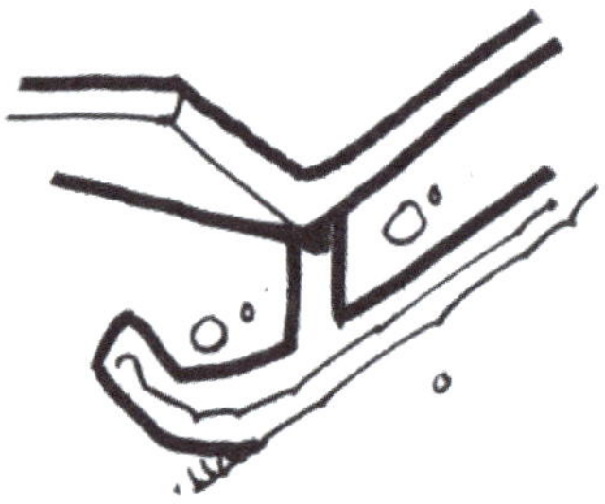 _____ (b)  _____ (c) _____

(d)  _____ (e)  _____ (f) _____

(g) 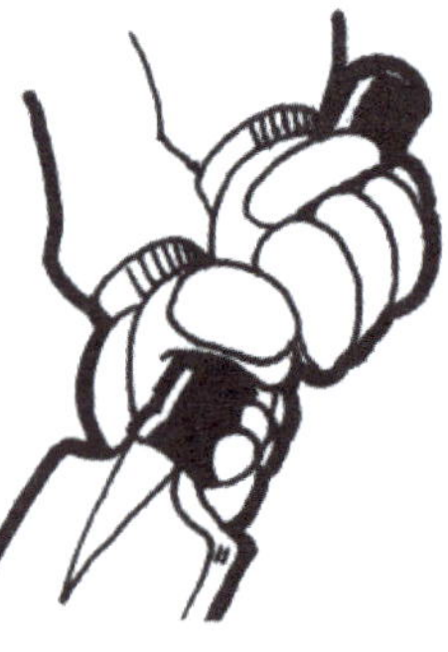 _____ (h) 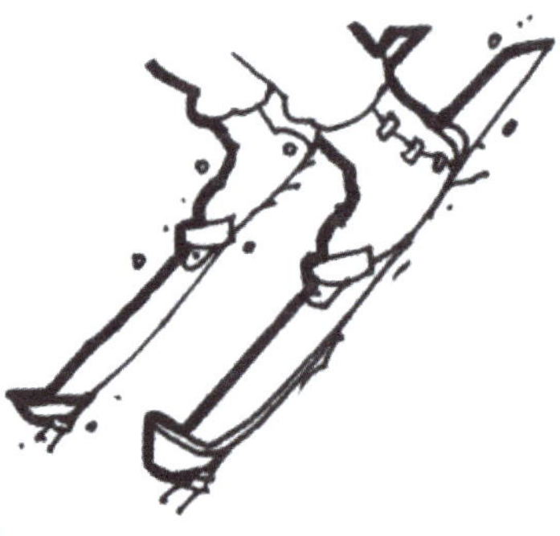 _____ (i) _____

2 For each of the high friction examples, write a sentence to say why high friction is needed.

_____

_____

_____

_____

3 Now do the same for the low friction examples.

_____

_____

_____

_____

4 The moving parts in a car engine need **low friction**. Why is this?

_____

_____

5 What is added to the engine to **reduce friction**?

_____

Car engines have lots of moving parts.

The engine needs something to make the parts slide easily.

Air brake

The force of the air pushes against the object.

Air resistance is a **force** which slows down objects that are moving through the air.

1 Look carefully at the pictures. Colour in the pictures that show the air slowing down an object.

(a) _____   (b) _____

(c) _____   (d) _____

(e) _____   (f) _____

2 Write a sentence under each picture you have coloured to explain what is happening.

3 Take two pieces of A4 paper. Hold them at arm's length like this and drop them at the same time.

Hold one piece horizontally.

Hold one piece vertically.

Look carefully at how they fall.

Describe how each piece of paper fell to the ground.

_____

_____

_____

_____

 On which piece of paper was the air resistance greater?

_____

Solids

These objects are all made out of **solid** materials.

_____ _____ _____ _____

_____ _____ _____ _____

  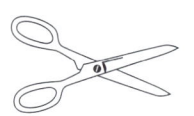 
_____ _____ _____ _____

1 Under each picture write down what the object is made of.

2 Solids have specific properties. Are the statements below always true, sometimes true or never true?

Write 'sometimes' or 'always' or 'never' next to each statement.

(a) A solid takes the shape of its container. _____

(b) A solid keeps its own shape. _____

(c) A solid is difficult to break. _____

(d) A solid sinks. _____

(e) A solid is heavy. _____

(f) A solid is shiny. _____

(g) A solid stays the same shape unless you do something to it.

_____

Liquids

Liquids are different from solids because they flow from place to place and take the shape of the container they are in.

 Mark buys his cola in these bottles.

 Melanie buys her cola in these bottles.

1 The cola bottles contain the same amount of liquid, but why does Mark's bottle look as if it contains more than Melanie's?

_____

_____

2 Melanie poured her cola into different containers. Colour the shape that the cola takes in each container.

Now try this test to see how liquids change shape.

You will need
- water
- selection of clear plastic containers of different shapes

What to do
1. Pour 100 ml of water into each container.
2. Look carefully at the shape of the water.

3 What two things do you notice?

_____

_____

Solids that are like liquids

Some **solids** are made up from very small pieces. This can make them **behave** like **liquids**.

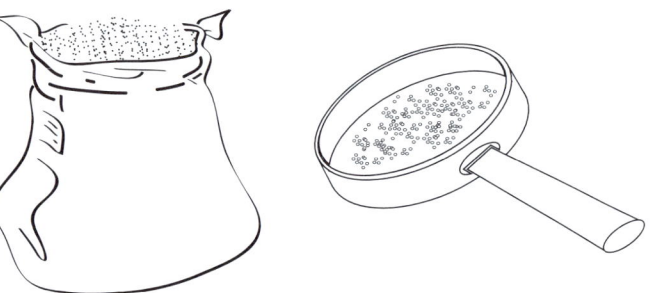

1. Look carefully at the following items under a magnifying glass. Draw what you see.

rice

sugar

salt

washing powder

instant coffee

2. How do these solids behave like liquids?

_____

_____

Left out

Some solids **melt** when they are heated.

A chocolate biscuit and a plain biscuit have been left in a warm place.

1. Describe what the biscuits look like.

_____

_____

Write Y for Yes. and N for No in the correct boxes.

2. Will any of these foods melt when they are heated?

Food	Melt Y or N	Food	Melt Y or N
Chocolate		Ice-lolly	
Bread		Cauliflower	
Ice-cream		Cheese	
Plain biscuit		Carrot	
Margarine		Sausage	
Pasta		Apple	

51

Melting and cooling

Solids **melt** at different temperatures.

This temperature is their melting point.

ice
0°C

ice-cream
−6°C

butter
16°C

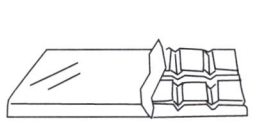
chocolate
36°C

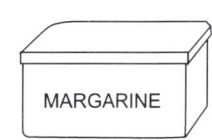
margarine
17°C

1 Record this information on a graph.

Take care with ice-cream.

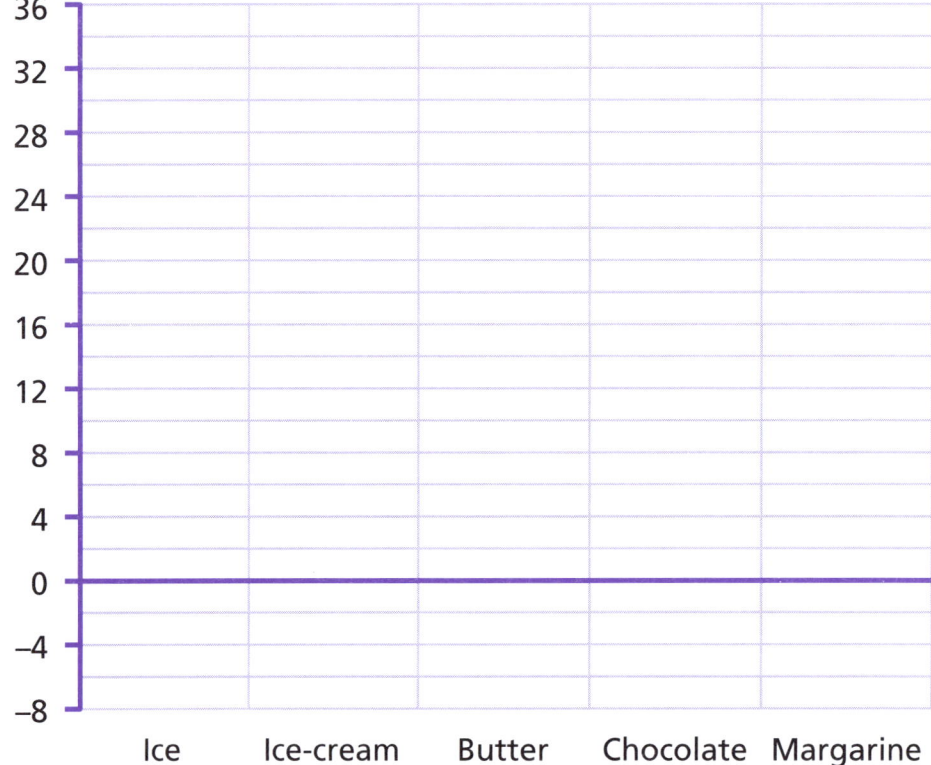

2 What happens when these melted solids **cool** down?

_____

Water

Some materials easily change from solid to liquid.
Water is one of these materials.

Water is a liquid. How can it be a solid too?

It is a solid when it is ice!

1 Explain how you can change liquid water into a solid or from a solid into a liquid. Write in the boxes.

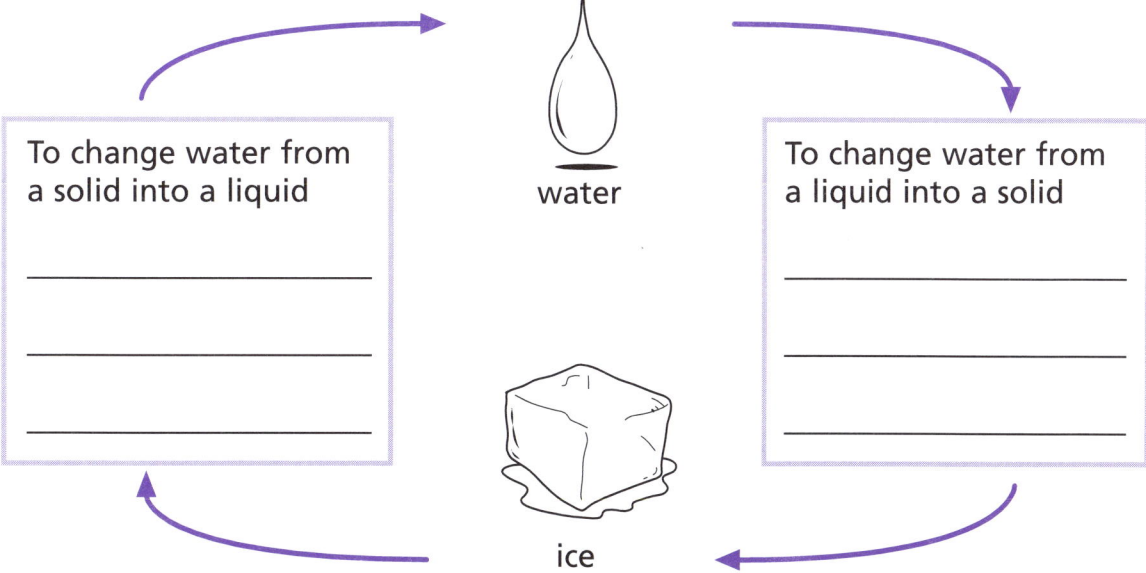

To change water from a solid into a liquid
_____
_____
_____

water

To change water from a liquid into a solid
_____
_____
_____

ice

2 Draw and label three pictures to show where you can find water as a liquid.

_____ _____ _____

3 Draw and label three pictures to show where you find water as a solid.

_____ _____ _____

Marvellous metals

Metals are very useful materials. They are used to make many different things in many different shapes and sizes.

Here are some things made of metal.

1 Make a list of some more things made of metal.

_____   _____   _____   _____

_____   _____   _____   _____

2 These stages show how metal is made into a useful material, but they are in the wrong order. Put the stages in the right order.

Write the number of the stage in the correct box.

The first stage has been done for you.

A chemical reaction takes place in the heat, producing liquid metal. The liquid metal takes the shape of the container.	

As the metal cools down it becomes a solid again.	

Pieces of the rock are taken to factories.	

Metals are found in rocks as ores.	1

Substances such as carbon are mixed with the rock. They are heated to very high temperatures in furnaces.	

3 In these sentences, the words **solid** and **liquid** have been missed out. Write the correct word in each gap.

(a) Metal can be shaped in many different ways when it is a

_____ .

When is metal a solid?

(b) When metal keeps its shape it is a _____ .

(c) When it is a _____ it takes the shape of the container it is put in.

When is metal a liquid?

(d) When metal is cool it becomes _____ and hard.

4 Write down six facts about metals. You can use the information on these pages to help you.

_____

_____

_____

_____

_____

_____

_____

_____

_____

_____

Mixed up

Things sometimes get **mixed up** when you don't want them to.

STONES
SAND

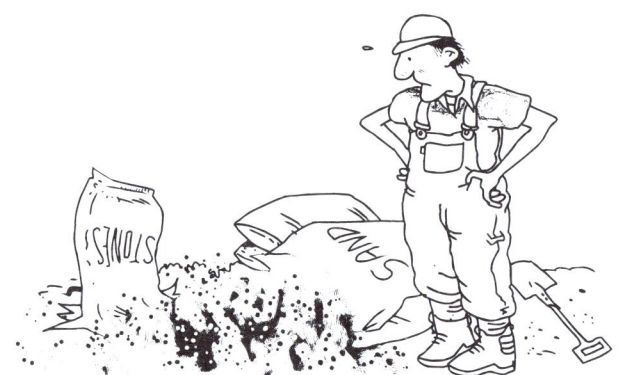

Which of these **sieves** would you use to separate the mixtures?

A 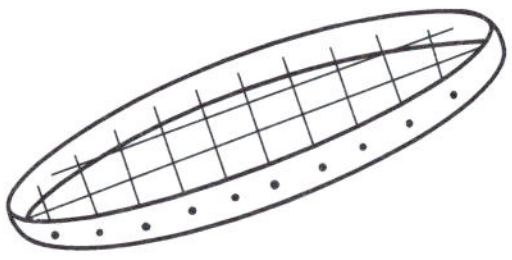 B 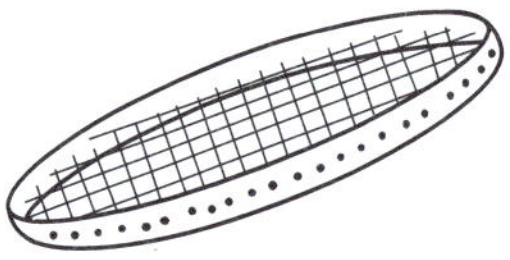 C 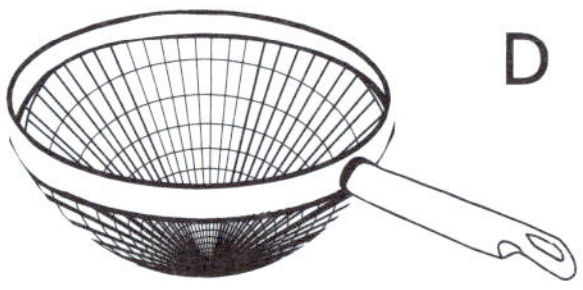 D 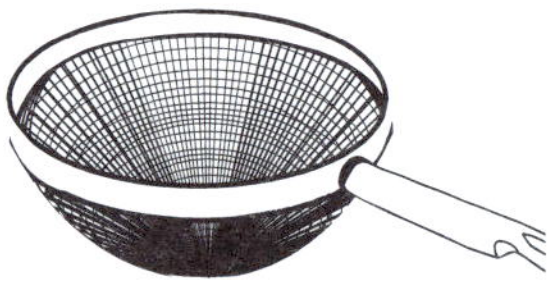

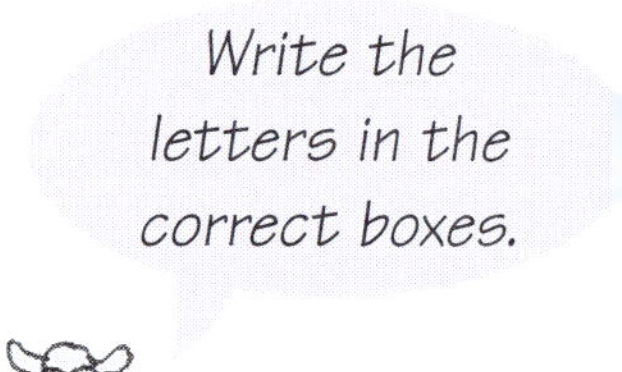
Write the letters in the correct boxes.

1 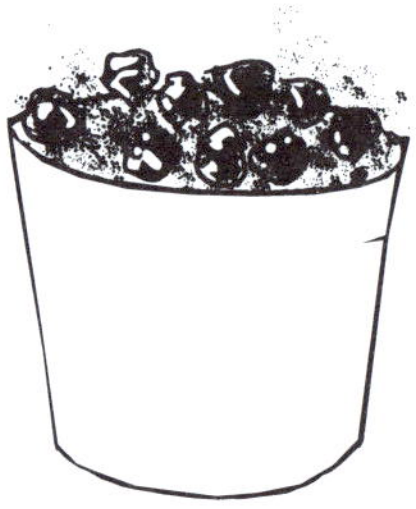

mixture of soil and stones ☐

2 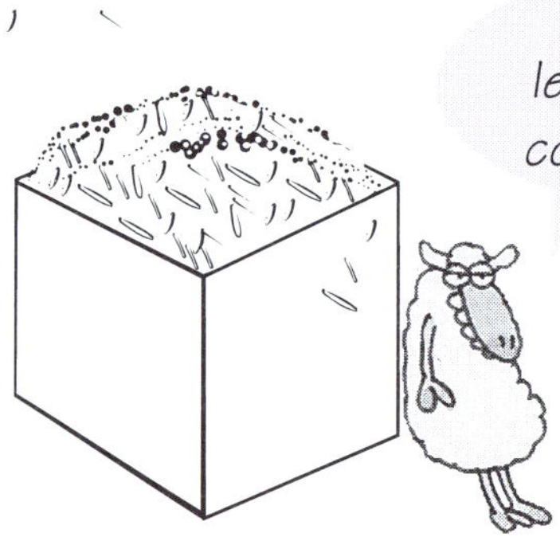

mixture of rice and flour ☐

3 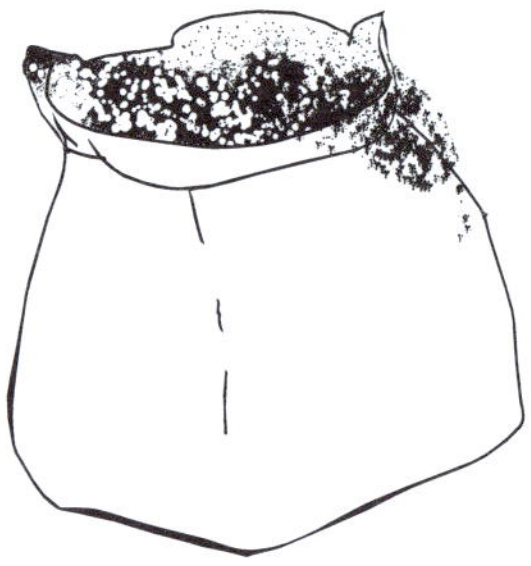

mixture of sand and gravel ☐

4 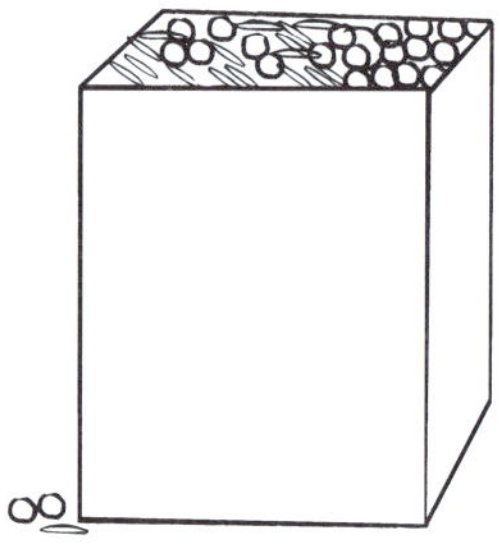

mixture of peas and rice ☐

5 Which of these mixtures could you separate using a sieve?

(a) marbles and sand

(d) pasta and flour

(b) salt and water

(e) water and sugar

(c) water and rice

What could you use to separate the mixtures that can't be separated using a sieve?

Which one would you separate first?

6 How would you separate a mixture of pasta, peas, rice and water into the four items?

_____

_____

_____

Disappearing solids

Rosie was experimenting to see which solids would **dissolve** in water. She put each solid into water and stirred for 30 seconds.

*If you cannot see the solid after you have stirred into the water, the solid has **dissolved**.*

Write either 'dissolve' or 'not dissolve'.

1 Make a prediction about what you think will happen when Rosie puts these solids in water.

Material + water	Prediction
salt	I think it will _____
sand	I think it will _____
sugar	I think it will _____
flour	I think it will _____
rice	I think it will _____
instant coffee	I think it will _____

Write your prediction in the correct space in the 'prediction' column.

2 Now test the solids to see if you were right. Sort the solids into these two groups:

Solids that did dissolve	Solids that did not dissolve

If you can still see the solid in the water, the solid has not dissolved.

58

Mystery solids

Lee had three solids but he didn't know their names. He tested them by mixing them with water as he thought this would help him to identify them!

> He put 100 ml of water into three pots.
> He added 20 g of solid A into jar A.
> He added 20 g of solid B into jar B.
> He added 20 g of solid C into jar C.

He stirred the water in each jar 10 times. Here are his results.

Jar A The solid dissolved into the water.	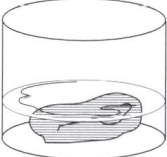 1
Jar B The solid started to disperse but there were some lumps on the bottom of the jar.	 2
Jar C The solid did not dissolve into the water and stayed on the bottom of the jar.	3

1 Draw a line to match the description with the correct drawing.

2 The solids were flour, salt and sand. Can you guess which was which?

Jar A _____   Jar B _____   Jar C _____

3 How did Lee make his test fair?

_____

_____

Lee did three things to make his test fair.

Changes

Some solids and liquids **change** when they are mixed with water, or when they are heated or cooled down.

1 Match the correct change to its meaning by drawing a line to join up the boxes.

solidify	when a solid turns into a liquid
melt	when a solid mixes with water leaving a clear liquid
freeze	when a liquid turns into a solid
dissolve	when a liquid turns into a solid because the temperature is so cold

2 Choose one of these words to explain what is about to happen in each picture. Write your choice below each picture.

melt   freeze   dissolve   solidify

(a) _____   (b) _____   (c) _____   (d) _____

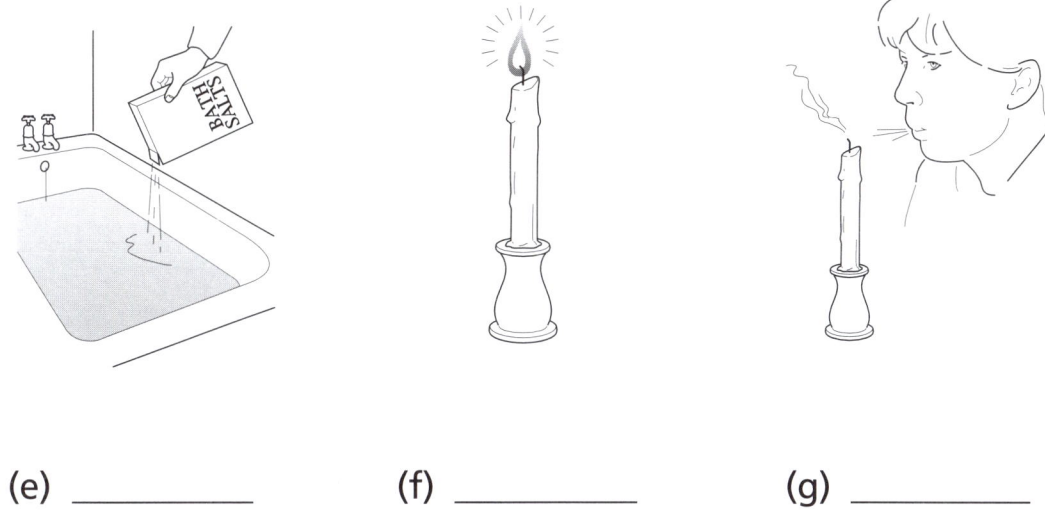

(e) _____   (f) _____   (g) _____

3 Here are some sentences about solids and liquids. Some of them are true, some are false.

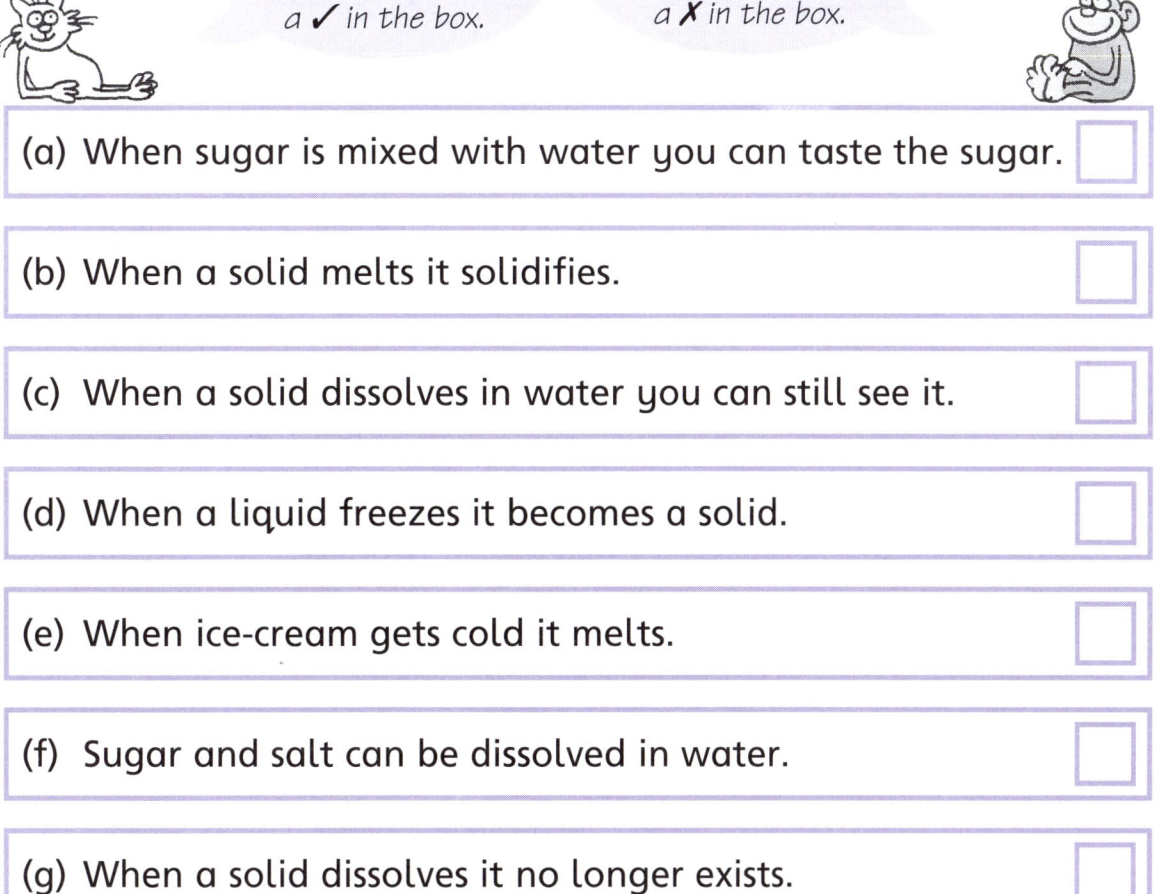

If you think the sentence is true, put a ✓ in the box.

If you think the sentence is false, put a ✗ in the box.

(a) When sugar is mixed with water you can taste the sugar. ☐

(b) When a solid melts it solidifies. ☐

(c) When a solid dissolves in water you can still see it. ☐

(d) When a liquid freezes it becomes a solid. ☐

(e) When ice-cream gets cold it melts. ☐

(f) Sugar and salt can be dissolved in water. ☐

(g) When a solid dissolves it no longer exists. ☐

Puzzler

Can you find a place in the grid for each of the science words below?

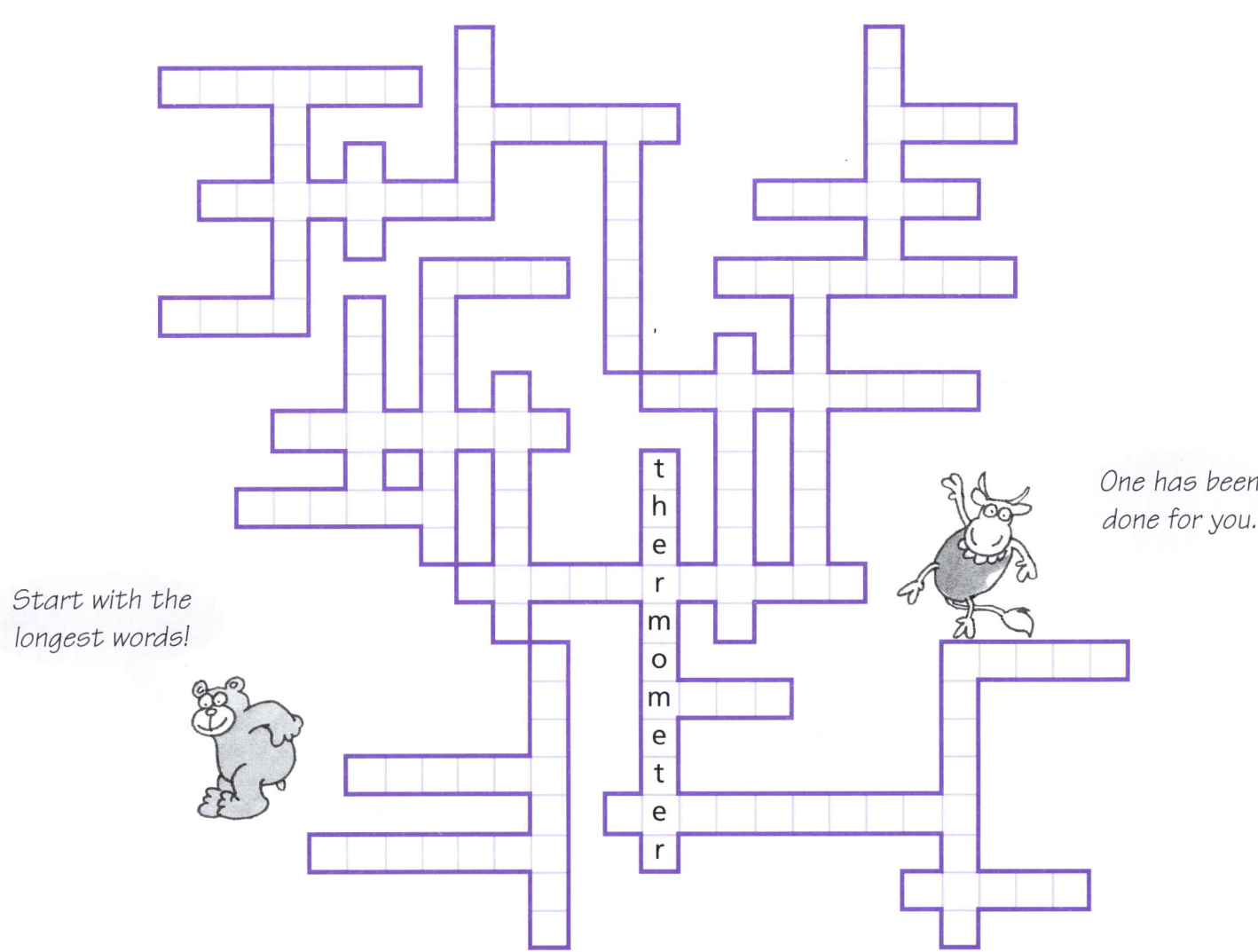

Start with the longest words!

One has been done for you.

3 letters
hot

4 letters
melt   prey   ribs   bulb

5 letters
skull   solid   spine

6 letters
freeze   liquid   change
switch   insect

7 letters
Celsius   conduct
degrees   habitat
muscles   circuit

8 letters
consumer   dissolve
friction   insulate
predator   producer
skeleton

9 letters
conductor
insulator

10 letters
vertebrate

11 letters
temperature

Answers and Hints

In some instances there may be more than one possible answer so you may need to check that the answer your child has given is reasonable. As long as your child's answer makes sense and has shown they understand the question, you should mark it right. Sometimes the question will ask them to express an opinion, to make a prediction or to create their own piece of work. When marking your child's efforts please remember that encouragement is always more helpful than criticism.

PAGE 5
1 (connected habitats and animals/plants) (pond) water lily, dragonfly, bullrushes, fish; (woodland) bluebell, deer, rabbit, owl, oak tree; (flower bed) rose, lavender, butterfly; (desert) camel, lizard, cactus   2 Check that your child has written some other examples of animals and plants that live in these habitats.

PAGES 6 & 7

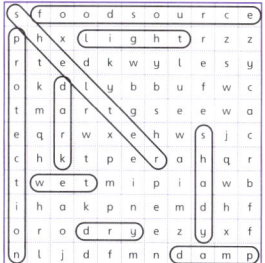

2 (b) dark, damp; (c) light, dry; (d) shady; (e) shady; (f) wet; (g) wet; (h) dark, damp; (i) wet, damp (If your child has written other or different conditions check if you think they are reasonable.)

PAGE 8
1 (goldfish) fish; (sparrow) birds; (mouse) mammals; (frog) amphibians; (snake) reptiles   2 (cold-blooded, ticked groups) fish, amphibians, reptiles; (warm-blooded) birds, mammals; (have moist skin) amphibians; (have scales) fish, reptiles; (have feathers) birds; (have fur or hair) mammals; (breathe through gills) fish, amphibians – when young; (breathe through lungs) amphibians, reptiles, birds, mammals; (lay eggs) fish, amphibians, reptiles, birds; (give birth to live young) mammals.

PAGE 9
1 (first column, top to bottom) swordfish, eagle, toad; (second column) mole, lizard   2 Check your child's clues – can you work out the animal they are thinking of?

PAGES 10 & 11
1 (with legs, no wings) millipede, ant, earwig, woodlouse, centipede, spider; (with legs and wings) moth, bee, beetle, wasp, housefly (all beetles actually have wings under their shells (like a ladybird) although some beetles never use them to fly) Your child should see that there are no minibeasts with wings but no legs (that area of the Venn diagram is empty).   2 snail   3 (wings, six legs) moth, bee, beetle, wasp, housefly (wings, not six legs) none (others: there are no minibeasts with wings that don't have six legs); (no wings, six legs) ant, earwig (others: flea); (no wings, not six legs) millipede, snail, woodlouse, centipede, spider (others: caterpillar, earthworm)   4 Check that your child has written any minibeasts of their own in the correct space on the diagram (other examples are given in the answer above).

PAGES 12 & 13
1 (left to right) bee, ant, snail, earthworm   2 (top question box) Does it have six legs?; (left question box) Does it have wings?; (right question box) Does it have eight legs?   3 (left to right) butterfly, earwig, spider, millipede.

PAGES 14 & 15
1 (numbers in boxes, left to right) (a) 3, 2, 1; (b) 2, 1, 3; (c) 3, 2, 1
2 (a) leaves, slug, hedgehog; (b) wheat, vole, owl; (c) cabbage leaf, caterpillar, bluetit.

PAGES 16 & 17
1 (a) leaf sap, aphid, ladybird; (b) algae, water flea, stickleback; (c) plant remains, earthworm, shrew   2 (filled in boxes on page 16, top to bottom) thrush, heron, buzzard   3 there would be fewer aphids; more ladybirds would probably also mean more thrushes (although thrushes do eat lots of other things as well)   4 the algae, water fleas and stickleback can only survive in the pond, so if the pond were drained they would all die; without any food to eat the heron would fly away to another pond.

PAGES 18 & 19
1 Check that your child has thought of sensible sentences to describe how hot or cold they feel at different times.   2 Check that your child has placed the descriptions in the correct order (from very cold to very hot, running up the thermometer).   3 (first row, left to right) 10 °C, 30 °C, 50 °C, 25 °C, 65 °C; (second row) 8 °C, −5 °C, 100 °C, 28 °C, −3 °C

PAGE 20
1 (kettle) 100 °C, (freezer) −10 °C, (beach) 25 °C, (winter scene) −3 °C (Check that your child has filled in the thermometers correctly.)
2 (cold to hot) −10 °C, −3 °C, 25 °C, 100 °C

PAGE 21
1 the temperature has gone down to 25 °C   2 Your child should understand that any object will cool down if placed somewhere that is cooler than the object (for example boiling water left at room temperature, or tap water left in a freezer). What is happening is that heat energy is moving from the object to the surrounding environment, but this is not a simple physical process. It is difficult for children at this age to say why this happens, but talk to them about their understanding of heat and cold and get them to explain it in their own words.
3 any number between 100 and 120 minutes should be marked correct
4 Your child should know that the ice will melt at room temperature, and understand that this process is the same process as that discussed in answer 2 (and that heat energy only moves from the hot thing (in this case the air) to the cool thing (the ice)).

PAGE 22
1 & 2 Check that you child has coloured the warm places red (cooker, radiator) and cool places blue (fridge, outside door).   3 Check your child's plan of a room – have they marked warm and cool places correctly?

PAGE 23
1 the temperature has increased   2 (left to right) wool, bubble wrap, felt, cotton   3 they used the same amount of insulation for each test (which used insulation), the same amount of drink in the same container, and made sure the drinks were the same temperature to start with.

PAGE 24
1 Check your child's drawing (they may have drawn a coat, a scarf, gloves, a jumper, etc.)   2 they are made from wool or thick cotton, which are good insulators   3 so the handles do not heat up too much
4 Check that your child has coloured the insulators red (oven gloves; thermos flask; man's hat and coat; dog's jacket).

PAGE 25

2 (a) true, (b) false, (c) false, (d) false, (e) true, (f) false.

PAGE 26
1 Check that your child has correctly spotted all the dangers (kite flying on to overhead wires, man pushing lawn mower towards cable, loose wall socket, child playing with exposed wall socket, woman pulling vacuum cable too tight, kettle lead left loose and sitting in water, frayed lead, overloaded wall socket)   2 8 (counting the individual dangers as listed above; your child may have counted them differently).

PAGE 27
1 shock   2 water   3 safe   4 wire   5 switch   6 electricity   7 fingers
8 light   9 Turn   10 socket   11 Too   The message reads 'safety first' – make sure your child understands the dangers of electricity.

PAGES 28 & 29
1 Your child should have coloured only bulb (a) yellow.   2 (a) bulb lights because the circuit is complete; (b) bulb doesn't light because one of the wires is missing; (c) bulb doesn't light because one of the wires isn't connected to the battery; (d) bulb doesn't light because the bulb is not screwed into its socket; (e) bulb doesn't light because both wires are connected to the same terminal on the socket; (f) bulb doesn't light because the switch is missing (there is a gap in the circuit)   3 (left to right) On, Off, Off   4 (possible answers) torch, television, ceiling light, desk lamp, computer, wall socket.

PAGES 30 & 31
1 (conductors, any order) metal fork, paper clip, 10p coin, aluminium foil
2 they are all made of metal   3 Check that your child has only listed metal things or things made from graphite (e.g. pencil lead).   4 Your child should have spotted that the light is on but isn't plugged in, there is no lead from the plug in the wall to the electric fire, the TV and video aren't connected, and no wire runs into the ceiling from the lamp shade.

PAGE 32
1 (insulators) B, C, E; (conductors) A, D, F   2 (correct statements) Pins and metal wires are conductors because the electricity has to flow through them for the plug to work properly. Plastic case and wire covering are insulators because otherwise you'd get a dangerous electric shock if you touched the plug or wire while it was turned on!

PAGE 33
1 (battery) torch, camera, radio-controlled car; (mains) microwave oven, portable television, kettle, table lamp, toaster, television, computer, fridge; (both) wall clock, radio   2 they need more electricity than batteries can supply   3 they only need a little electricity; using batteries allow them to be portable (don't have to be plugged in); mains electricity would break them (they might even explode!) – they would need adapters to make them work.

PAGE 34
1 (a) gull; (b) fish; (c) snake; (d) monkey; (e) wallaby; (f) deer 2 box (e) (although your child might have said box (d) because humans can climb trees!)

PAGE 35
1 (missing labels, left side, top to bottom) skull, shoulder blade, rib, thigh bone; (right side) jaw, collar bone, spine, knee cap 2 thigh bone 3 Check your child's extra labels – have they labelled any of the other bones correctly? 4 (a) ribs; (b) spine; (c) skull.

PAGE 36
1 (underlined words) hard, light, strong, smooth 2 (correct animals) (a) bird, (b) fish, (c) snake, (d) frog, (e) cat 3 all the skeletons have spines (back bones) 4 Check your child's drawing – discuss the drawing with them if you think any part of it is wrong.

PAGE 37
1 (possible answers) run, skip, bend down, stretch, spin round, dance, climb, forward roll, handstand 2 (possible answers) tired, aching, hot, out of breath 3 (a) they have been worked hard (pulled and stretched) (b) breathing is faster; (c) heartbeat is faster.

PAGE 38
1 (animals coloured red) lobster, whelk, stag beetle, prawn, woodlouse, cockle 2 (animals coloured blue) leech, jellyfish, lugworm, slug.

```
s h r i m p v i d o s
b u a s i w c w a s p
k l f l y e s m e h i
c d r a s w a c a u d
r k b c g w o y n o e
a l e f l o b s t e r
b e e h s r t o z i d
r e t a w m u s s e l
f c l o p x r t l e d
w h e l k c h i u b a
g r u y b u b u g e n
```

PAGE 39
Matched animals and descriptions: worm–has no skeleton and no legs..., centipede–has a hard, outer skeleton and about 30 legs..., ladybird–has an outer skeleton including a set of hard, red wing cases..., crab–has a very hard outer skeleton with jointed legs..., woodlouse–has a jointed outer skeleton..., snail–has a coiled shell...

PAGES 40 & 41
1 (a) pull, (b) twist, (c) push, (d) pull, (e) twist, (f) push, (g) pull, (h) twist 2 Check that your child has drawn an arrow on each picture to indicate the direction of the push, pull or twist in each case.
3 (possible answers, push) pushing a swing or pushchair; (pull) removing a plug from a socket or a key from a lock; (twist) turning car window handles or temperature dials on ovens.

PAGES 42 & 43
1 Check that your child has completed the bar chart correctly, by adding the numbers on the vertical axis (6, 8, 10, 12, 14, 16), filling in the blank boxes on the horizontal axis (vinyl, wood) and adding bars at heights corresponding to (left to right) 14, 12, 12, 13, 10, 10, 9, 10, 9, 8, 9, 9
2 wood 3 Your child should understand that experiments are often repeated several times to allow average results to be calculated. This process can remove the effects of any small changes in the results due to human error, slightly inaccurate measuring of amounts, and variations in room temperature (and other 'environmental' factors).

PAGES 44 & 45
1 (a) high frictions, (b) low friction, (c) high friction, (d) low friction, (e) high friction, (f) high friction, (g) low friction, (h) high friction, (i) low friction 2 (goalkeeper gloves) gloves need to grip the ball well so that the goalkeeper doesn't drop it!; (car tyre) tyre needs to grip the road to push car along; (trainer sole) shoe needs to grip the floor so the runner doesn't slip over; (cycle brakes) brakes need to grip wheel to slow it down; (cricket gloves) gloves need to grip bat to allow the cricketer to swing the bat without dropping it 3 (sled runner) needs to slide through snow without slowing the sled down; (children's slide) needs to let the children slide down fast; (rollerblades) wheels need to turn easily to let the rollerblader move along easily; (skis) need to slide over the snow without slowing the skier down 4 they move over and through each other a lot and would wear out quickly (and get too hot and possible start to melt) if they rubbed against each other 5 motor oil.

PAGES 46 & 47
1 Your child should have coloured in pictures (a), (d) and (f).
2 (possible written explanations) (a) the woman cannot walk quickly since the wind is pushing against her and her umbrella, (d) the wind is pushing against the man on the bicycle, making it more difficult for him to cycle forward, (f) the air is catching in the parachute, pulling backwards on the car 3 Check your child's description of how the paper fell – the flat piece should have fallen more slowly, but both pieces would have curled up and neither would have fallen straight down.
4 flat piece.

PAGE 48
1 (bottle) glass/plastic, (chair) wood, (fork) metal, (tumbler) glass/plastic, (coat hanger) metal/wood, (key) metal, (step ladder) wood/metal, (pencil) wood/graphite, (saucepan) metal, (ruler) wood/plastic, (scissors) metal, (table) wood (Most of the objects are often made out of several different materials, so you should mark any sensible answer correct.)
2 (a) never true; (b) always true; (c) sometimes true; (d) sometimes true; (e) sometimes true; (f) sometimes true; (g) always true.

PAGE 49
1 Mark's bottle is taller than Melanie's 2 Check that your child has coloured in the containers correctly; the colour should fill the inside of the container and be drawn with a level top. 3 liquids always take the shape of the container, and always have a level surface.

PAGE 50
1 Check your child's drawings – talk to them about the shapes and sizes of the different substances. 2 the small pieces can run over each other (they can be poured like liquids) and can fill up different shaped containers.

PAGE 51
1 the chocolate on the chocolate biscuit has become runny, the plain biscuit hasn't changed 2 (does it melt?, first column) Y, N, Y, N, Y, N; (second column) Y, N, Y, N, N, N.

PAGE 52
1 Check that your child has completed the bar chart correctly (at heights corresponding to (left to right) 0, –6, 16, 36 and 17; the 0 bar could be drawn as a thick line along the horizontal axis, the –6 bar must be drawn below this axis) 2 they will all turn back to solids if cooled below their melting points

PAGE 53
1 Your child should understand that water changes to ice when it is frozen (in a freezer, for instance) and that ice turns to water when it is heated above 0 °C (holding it in your hands will melt ice, or leaving out at room temperature). 2 (possible answers) swimming pool, dew drops, puddle 3 (possible answers) North or South pole, snowy mountains, snow and hail storms.

PAGES 54 & 55
1 (possible answers) airplanes, cars, boats, door hinges, some furniture, some spectacle frames (Check that any answer your child suggests can (sometimes) be made of metal.) 2 (correct order) 2–Pieces of the rock..., 3–Substances such as carbon..., 4–A chemical reaction..., 5–As the metal cools down... 3 (missing words, in order) liquid, solid, liquid, solid 4 they are strong, they are cold to the touch, most are shiny, they are difficult to break, they keep their shape when solid, they can be melted and made into different shapes (Your child may have written some different facts, but mark them correct provided they are sensible.)

PAGES 56 & 57
1 A 2 D 3 B 4 C 5 mixtures (a), (c), (d) could be separated using a sieve 6 use three different size sieves to separate out first the water, then the rice and then the peas (the pasta would be left in the third sieve).

PAGE 58
1 Check that you child has completed a prediction for each mixture.
2 (solids that did dissolve) salt, sugar, instant coffee; (solids that did not dissolve) sand, flour, rice.

PAGE 59
1 (connected descriptions and pictures) A–2, B–3, C–1 2 (jar A) salt, (jar B) flour, (jar C) sand 3 he used the same amount of solid and water (at the same temperature) in each case, and stirred the jars the same amount.

PAGES 60 & 61
1 (connected words and meanings) solidify–when a liquid turns into a solid..., melt–when a solid turns into a liquid, freeze–when a liquid turns into a solid, dissolve–when a solid mixes with water... 2 (a) freeze, (b) solidify, (c) dissolve, (d) melt, (e) dissolve, (f) melt, (g) solidify
3 (top to bottom) true, false, false, true, false, true, false.

PAGE 62

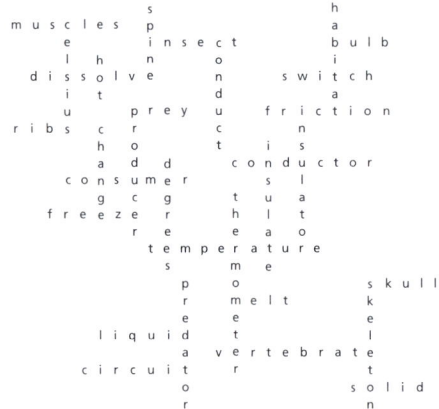